The Advanced Guide to REAL ESTATE INVESTING

How to Identify the Hottest Markets and Secure the Best Deals

Ken McElroy

BUSINESS PLUS

NEW YORK   BOSTON

CASHFLOW, Rich Dad, Rich Dad's Advisors, Rich Dad's Seminars, EBSI, B-I Triangle are registered trademarks of CASHFLOW Technologies, Inc.

E B   E|B
S I   S|I

Business Plus
Hachette Book Group USA
237 Park Avenue
New York, NY 10017

Visit our Web sites at www.HachetteBookGroupUSA.com and www.richdad.com.

Business Plus is an imprint of Grand Central Publishing.
The Business Plus name and logo are trademarks of Hachette Book Group USA, Inc.

Printed in the United States of America

First Edition: May 2008

10 9 8 7 6 5 4 3 2 1

Library of Congress Cataloging-in-Publication Data

McElroy, Ken.
   The advanced guide to real estate investing : how to identify the hottest markets and secure the best deals / Ken McElroy.—1st ed.
      p.   cm.—(Rich dad's advisors)
   ISBN-13: 978-0-446-53832-9
   ISBN-10: 0-446-53832-9
   1. Real estate investment.   2. Real estate investment—handbooks, manuals, etc.
I. Title.   II. Series.
HD1382.5.M2952   20084
332.63'24—dc22

                                                    2008000501

Acknowledgments

For all the employees of MC Companies, thank you for your continued dedication and loyalty. A special thanks to Jake Johnson for helping with the process—finally, you get to apply your college degree to something.

Contents

"Wealth is the ability to fully experience life." —HENRY DAVID THOREAU

"Landlords grow rich in their sleep." —JOHN STUART MILL

"Buying real estate is not only the best way, the quickest way,
the safest way, but the only way to become wealthy." —MARSHALL FIELD

"Every person who invests in well-selected real estate in a growing section of
a prosperous community adopts the surest and safest method of becoming
independent, for real estate is the basis of wealth." —THEODORE ROOSEVELT

Foreword

by Robert Kiyosaki

In my book *Rich Dad's Increase Your Financial IQ*, I relate a story about getting ready for an interview with a morning news program in early August 2007, right after the Dow had crashed by nearly 400 points. In response, the Fed and central banks around the world had infused the economy with billions in cash in an effort to soothe investors' nerves. That morning the television pundits were weighing in on the state of the economy. One financial advisor who was being interviewed said that the crash didn't change her advice to her clients: avoid real estate because it's too risky and invest in blue chip stocks and mutual funds over the long term.

There is a stark difference between the way that professional money pundits think and my own philosophy. Financial planners and the so-called experts will always tell you "Save money, get out of debt, and invest for the long term in a well-diversified portfolio of stocks, bonds, and mutual funds." They refer to this type of investing as "safe" while denouncing other investments such as real estate as "risky."

While I was watching the interview with this financial planner, my wife, Kim, came into the room and reminded me that we had a closing scheduled for a 300-unit apartment building later that day. Both Kim and I were excited to be closing on this building, and we both knew it was going to be a tremendous investment.

As I slipped on my suit jacket, I couldn't help but smile, thinking about what the financial planner being interviewed had said. All of the investments that she considered to be safe, I actually considered to be risky. Why? Because what she really meant by safe investments are in actuality low-yield investments that often barely keep pace with inflation, if at all. That means that placing—parking—my money in those types of investments is not financially intelligent, because while it may seem like my money will have grown over time, it will, in reality, have only maintained its value.

In the Rich Dad company, we believe in investing with financial intelligence. Part of developing your financial intelligence is to surround yourself with people who are smarter than you and to learn everything you can from them. That is the very concept behind the Rich Dad's Advisor series. The 300-unit apartment building investment opportunity I mentioned earlier was brought to me by my good friend, and Rich Dad's Advisor, Ken McElroy.

Many years ago, I decided to seek out the best advisors to increase my financial IQ, and Ken McElroy was the natural choice when it came to real estate. Besides being a superior golfer, Ken also holds superior knowledge when it comes to the intricacies and know-how of real estate investing. He owns one of the most respected property management, real estate investment, and development companies in the Southwest and has been working as a real estate professional since he graduated from college. He is a former president of the Arizona Multifamily Housing Association and board member for the National Apartment Association, and he is active in lobbying Congress for the real estate industry. But above all, Ken is a phenomenal teacher whose passion is to see others—people like you who are reading this book—become financially independent.

For many of you, this will not be your first exposure to Ken and his teachings on real estate investing. Ken has already written one book for the Rich Dad company, *The ABC's of Real Estate Investing*, which is a bestseller, and he is a frequent speaker and teacher at Rich Dad events.

If this *is* your first exposure to Ken, however, you are in for a treat. Often-times people feel investing in real estate is risky simply because they don't really understand the secrets that make investing in real estate not only prof-itable but also safe. I asked Ken to write this book because I felt that at this time in our economic history, it is very important to become educated in how to succeed in an increasingly confusing economy. Ken, as always, takes seem-ingly complicated information and makes it simple to understand and excit-ing to think about.

Lately I've been talking a lot about currency—U.S. currency, to be spe-cific. In 1971, Nixon took the U.S. dollar off the gold standard for good. At that point the U.S. dollar ceased to be money and became currency. Currency in and of itself has no inherent value. It is simply a tool to be manipulated. Just like an electric current, currency needs to travel from one point to another or else it dies. Because of Nixon's policy, savers have become losers. History proves that all currencies lose value and become worthless. The longer you hold on to your currency, the less valuable it will become.

The real winners in today's economy are the ones who understand that real value is found in assets, not dollars. I'm convinced that one of the best assets your money can buy is real estate. In this book, Ken shows you the secrets of a real estate investor and how real estate as an asset class has the potential to create vast amounts of wealth, wealth that can make you finan-cially free.

When I look to make a real estate investment, I turn to my advisor Ken McElroy. He is an invaluable resource to me. You too have the opportunity, through Ken's book and his teachings, to put his valuable experience and expertise to work in your real estate investments. I commend you for taking the opportunity to further educate yourself and beginning your path toward financial freedom. I promise you will not be disappointed, because the depth and quality of Ken's knowledge of real estate investing is top-notch. In this book, he truly is sharing with you the advanced secrets of a successful real estate investor.

Why Not Just Follow the Wealthy?

It took me a long time to get to the place where I am today. Just like you, I spent a good portion of my working life trying to earn more money so I could spend it on more things. Slowly, through many years of trial and error, I earned my stripes on the job. But I was still working for others. My money was dependent on others.

Success or excellence in any field or subject depends on a combination of "doing things right and doing the right things at the right time." You need a combination of activities and efforts in a specific area of interest to achieve real expertise. Just look at the people at the top. What do *they* do? What makes them successful?

I am constantly learning and seeking out better ways to do things. For instance, I have several mentors that I meet with every month. They are further along the path of life than I am, and I look to them for leadership and advice. I study people's habits and practices, and I try to implement them into my habits and life. Also, I belong to an association of business owners and entrepreneurs, whose purpose of getting together is to problem-solve, and share ideas and thoughts at the top level of highly successful organizations.

Many of you are going through the same process I went through. I commend you for picking up this book, as well as other *Rich Dad* books, and educating yourself. If you continue to learn, and to apply your learning by investing in assets, you, too, will be financially free. Once you have the knowledge, all successful real estate investing requires is common sense. Equipped with knowledge and the insider tips in this book you will be able to use your common sense when evaluating a deal. There will be no magic, just know-how.

Then, with that as the foundation, I will spend the rest of the book teaching you how to acquire a multifamily property of your own. We'll cover the search process, how to finance your investment, finding a team and investors, due diligence, legal setup, and more. I'll walk you through a large multifamily acquisition all the way to the closing table. By the end of the book, you will feel equipped and confident to find, acquire, and operate your own multifamily investment.

So, how do we get started? Let's follow the wealthy. Because *now* is the time to create your future, and your future will be determined by the choices you make and the commitments that you honor.

Who Are the Wealthy?

Every year *Forbes* magazine puts out a list of the 400 wealthiest Americans. I know it may come as a surprise but I'm not on this list. But there are plenty of people you would recognize, and a lot more you've never heard of. Amazingly, in 2007 there are only billionaires on this list. That marks the first time in the history of the *Forbes* Richest Americans list that millionaires are excluded. More than 10 percent of the billionaires on the *Forbes* list earned their wealth from real estate. This is a phenomenal percentage, considering *Forbes* uses twenty different industry categories to determine wealth generation.

> Of the 400 billionaires on the *Forbes* Richest Americans list, 10 percent derived their wealth directly from real estate.

The two richest real estate tycoons on the list are Donald Bren and Samuel Zell. Both of these men are primarily known for their multifamily real estate investments and are proof that the best real estate investment around is apartment buildings.

DONALD BREN

As chairman of The Irvine Company, Bren's net worth is $13 billion, and he owns over 25,000 apartment units. The Irvine Company operates in Southern California and is known for its luxury and master planned communities. The company was founded by James Irvine in 1864 as a holding for his ranch acreage. Today the company's portfolio includes 400 office buildings, forty retail centers, ninety apartment communities, two hotels, five marinas, and three golf clubs. The company is privately held to this day and has propelled Bren into the category of one of the richest men in the world by virtue of its real estate holdings.

SAMUEL ZELL

Samuel Zell, at a net worth of $6 billion, is the founder of Equity Residential. He started the business in 1969 by managing apartment buildings in Michigan while he was in college. He has grown his company into the largest publicly traded owner, operator, and developer of multifamily housing in the United States.

In 1993 his company became one of the first real estate companies to go public. His company is listed on the S&P 500, and he is considered the godfather of public real estate companies. All of this was generated through multifamily investment. The company's annual return continually outperforms the Dow Jones Industrial Average and S&P 500 by multiple percentage points.

According to its public report, Equity Residential owns over 920 apartment buildings, comprising of 197,404 individual units. The company employs over 6,000 people. Recent operating revenues from the Equity apartment portfolio equaled $1.95 billion. The total asset value of their multifamily holdings equaled $16.6 billion.

Real Estate = Wealth

While 10 percent is a very strong showing for real estate on the *Forbes* list, what is not indicated is that even those who haven't derived their wealth directly from real estate still owe much of their success to real estate. For many, business ideas created enough liquidity to be able to invest in real estate.

Having read *Rich Dad, Poor Dad,* you know the classic example for this principle is McDonald's. In the book, Robert Kiyosaki tells the story of Ray Kroc, the founder of McDonald's, speaking to an MBA class. When he asked the students what business he was in, the amused class responded, hamburgers, of course. Kroc replied, "Ladies and gentlemen, I'm not in the hamburger business. My business is real estate."

The retail part of McDonald's business is only part of the picture. A huge part of the McDonald's success is their real estate holdings. According to a recent annual report, the total asset value of McDonald's real estate holdings is $29.9 billion. That is compared to their net operating income of $4 billion. As Robert writes, McDonald's is one of the largest owners of real estate in the world. The McDonald's business creates liquidity, but it's the McDonald's real estate that creates wealth. McDonald's is an obvious example of this concept, used by almost everyone teaching it. Let's take a look at some less obvious examples. I think you'll begin to see a pattern develop.

> **Business creates liquidity; real estate creates wealth.**

SHELDON ADELSON

To most people, Sheldon Adelson is known for being the founder of the Las Vegas Sands Corporation. The company owns huge casinos in Las Vegas such as the Venetian, and others throughout the world. Adelson was named the third richest person in America and the fifth richest person in the world by *Forbes,* with a net worth of $28 billion.

While it may be true that he gained his wealth through the gaming industry, the fact of the matter is that Adelson's true wealth comes from the real estate holdings of his company. The Las Vegas Strip is some of the most valuable real estate in the world. Depending on location, as of this writing, real estate on the Strip is selling for approximately $10 million to $20 million per acre. Again, a look at annual public reports reveals that the Las Vegas Sands Corporation's wealth is really in its real estate holdings. Their operations in 2005 netted them $589 million. Conversely, their real estate as-

WHY NOT JUST FOLLOW THE WEALTHY?

sets

are valued at $2.6 billion. Which would you rather own, the company or the land?

WALLY WORLD

The most dramatic example of a major company's wealth being concentrated in real estate is the story of the Walton family, the descendants of Wal-Mart founder Sam Walton. If Sam Walton were alive today, he would be the richest person in the entire world. In fact, it is estimated that his net worth would be double that of Bill Gates. The Walton family comprises over 40 percent of the top ten richest Americans. Many people know Sam Walton's success story. What they don't know is his failure story.

Walton started his first store in 1945 in Newport, Arkansas. That store is where he pioneered his operating philosophy that made his retail business so successful—buying wholesale and passing the savings on to his customers. There is no doubt that Walton's retail philosophy made him a great success. What many people don't know, however, is that he lost his first store because he didn't own the land or the building that he was operating in. The store was so successful that the landlord wouldn't renew the lease and forced a takeover on Walton.

Today, Wal-Mart is one of the largest real estate owners in the world. Their public reports indicate that they own over 800 million square feet of retail space in 6,779 locations. The company's total asset wealth is listed as $138 billion and property holdings are a whopping 57 percent of that total asset worth *after depreciation*. Just the land the buildings sit on is reported to have an asset value of $16 billion. That is equal to Microsoft co-founder Paul Allen's total net worth.

Wal-Mart's real estate holdings are so extensive that the company actually started their own realty company to manage them. Its slogan is "That's right. We sell land, too." The genius of this company is it feeds off the Wal-Mart name to create value. When the company is buying land to build a store on, they often purchase the adjoining land and sell it to developers who want to build next to a Wal-Mart. Just by the presence of their stores they create enormous value in the land. Additionally, they have hundreds of thousands of retail space near their existing stores that they lease out to other businesses like fast food chains and banks. A close look at Wal-Mart will tell you that Sam Walton may have started his fortune through retail, but it is sustained by real estate holdings. Today, the Waltons are the richest family in the world.

PAUL ALLEN

For companies like Wal-Mart and McDonald's, real estate may sustain the company's wealth, but they still carry on with operations as the sole focus of their business. For others, however, real estate becomes the primary focus of their business after they have generated wealth in other areas. Such is the case for Paul Allen.

Allen's net worth according to the *Forbes* list is estimated to be about $16.8 billion and he is the eleventh richest person in America. Allen is the co-founder of Microsoft. He represents one of four people on the *Forbes* 400 list who attribute their wealth to software, a number that is dramatically smaller than in years past, due to the popping of the tech bubble.

Allen retired from Microsoft in 1983. He owned about a quarter of the company's stock. Over the years he has been selling his shares in Microsoft and investing the earnings. In 1986, he founded Vulcan Northwest, Inc., and began placing his money in diversified investments. Through Vulcan he purchased controlling stakes in both the Portland Trail Blazers NBA team and the Seattle Seahawks NFL franchise. In 1992, he began plans for the Seattle rock music museum the Experience Music Project. Ever since he has been focusing his company's resources on building a substantial real estate portfolio through his subsidiary company Vulcan Real Estate.

According to Allen's public relations firm, current highlights for the company are, but not limited to, lead development roles in all construction projects, including:

- Three million square feet in the development pipeline.
- 900,000 square feet currently under construction, worth $300 million.
- Three new mixed-use residential projects totaling 672,599 square feet.
- 259 newly constructed, presold condominiums at a total value of $138.5 million.
- Medical Plaza for the University of Washington, which will total 284,000 square feet.

Not bad for a guy who dropped out of college. Before the tech bubble burst, there were a lot of millionaires on paper, but those "riches" came falling down like a house of cards. One key to Allen's success was that he moved his money from stocks into real estate, while those in the software industry who didn't, dropped out of existence.

World Powers

Real estate as a means to generate and sustain wealth is not simply an American concept. Each year *Forbes* also publishes a list of the world's wealthiest people. Again, 10 percent of this list is comprised of real estate investors—six of whom are among the 100 wealthiest people in the world. Some of the world's biggest real estate investors are based in Hong Kong.

LEE SHAU KEE

Lee Shau Kee is considered the twenty-second richest person in the world at a net worth of $17 billion. He is the founder and CEO of Henderson Land Development Company. His company is the largest land development company in Asia, with over $27 billion in total land asset value. The total asset value of the company is $66.6 billion.

Lee also sits on the board of the Sun Hung Kai company, which is owned by the second wealthiest landowners in the world, the Kwok brothers.

THE KWOK BROTHERS

Raymond, Thomas, and Walter Kwok are co-owners of Sun Hung Kai, one of the largest land companies in Hong Kong. Their net worth is $15 billion. They inherited the company from their father, who started it in 1969.

Today the company specializes in residential and commercial development, employing over 28,000 people in Hong Kong. They are partnered with Lee Shau Kee. Together they are building the International Commerce Center, which, upon its completion, will be the tallest building in Hong Kong, and the fourth largest in the world, at 118 stories.

In 2006, property sales and rental income *alone* amounted to $16 billion for the company, and its total land asset value is an astounding $133 billion.

The Playground of the Rich

By now you're probably thinking to yourself, "I thought this book was supposed to be about purchasing an apartment building, not a biography of the world's real estate moguls." But financial education is not just about knowing the numbers, it's also knowing the players. It should be clear from the case studies in this section that the true path to wealth and financial freedom is through real estate, the playground of the rich. Take a look at the accompanying chart. It's quite telling. These revenues and values were all derived from the companies' annual reports to the shareholders. As you can see, it is rather conclusive: "Business creates liquidity, real estate creates wealth."

	Company Revenues	*Real Estate Asset Value*
Kroc	$4 billion	$29.9 billion
Bren	Private	Private
Zell	$1.95 billion	$16.6 billion
Adelson	$589 million	$2.6 billion
Walton family	$3.2 billion	$78.7 billion
Allen	Private	Private
Kee	$10.9 billion	$66.7 billion
Kwok family	$25.5 billion	$133 billion

Before we get into the nuts and bolts of investing in apartment buildings, let's explore how doing so can change your life and your net worth, both for the better. In the next chapter, I will show you the advantages of real estate over any other type of investment. Once we have laid the foundation for the power of real estate as a whole, I'll show you why I feel multifamily investment in particular is the single greatest real estate investment available.

Chapter 1

The Power of Real Estate:
Ten Advantages

Don't Believe the Hype

Real estate is the ultimate investment. Nothing else provides the same kind of dollar-for-dollar returns and has the same kinds of advantages. If I had a choice to invest $1 million in real estate or $1 million in Microsoft stock, I would choose real estate, hands down. The reason is simple: Even if the real estate investment appreciated at half the rate as the stock, I would still come out way ahead when taking into account leverage, tax advantages, and cash flow. In this chapter I'll explain these advantages in detail.

This line of thinking runs counter to mainstream thought on investing in this country. As consumers, we are constantly barraged with articles, commercials, and advice to invest our money in stocks, bonds, or mutual funds. If you pick up any major investment publication, it's very likely you'll see articles touting the advantages of mutual funds and the stock market, while downplaying the viability of real estate as an investment tool. Coincidence? Not to my mind. I believe it has a great deal to do with the fact that the source of much of these publications' revenue comes from financial services companies that specialize in stocks, bonds, and mutual funds.

Just recently I picked up a copy of *Money* magazine because I saw that there was an article comparing the advantages of stocks vs. real estate. Although I already had a pretty good guess as to who it was going to pick as the winner before I read the article, I was curious to see how it reached its conclusion. In the article, "Real Estate vs. Stocks," which appeared in the May 2007 issue, the author creates eight "rounds" for the two investment types to "box." Not surprisingly, stocks come out on top most of the time.

Round 1:   Performance—Historical gains

Round 2:   Leverage—Using Other People's Money

Round 3:   Costs—Costs associated with the transaction such as commissions and fees

Round 4:   Taxes—Tax benefits available through each investment

Round 5:   Transparency—Being able to see hidden traps

Round 6:   Effort—The amount of time involved in managing the investment

Round 7:   Volatility—How quickly the investment can rise or fall in value

Round 8:   Diversification—Not putting all your eggs in one basket

The author uses a boxing match as a metaphor for the article, but it reads more like a staged professional wrestling match in which the winner is already picked before the match begins.

As an interesting exercise, I went through the same issue of the magazine that this article appears in and counted the number of ads for financial institutions. They accounted for one-third of the total number of advertising pages for the magazine. By obtaining the advertising rate schedule and doing some math, I found that these companies could have paid approximately $3,777,025 for ad placement in this issue. As I read through the article I began to question more and more whether the magazine's advertisers could be influencing its content. While there were some truths, there were a number of places that left me scratching my head. Here is one example:

The centerpiece of the article is a chart entitled, "How Profitable Is That

House?," which sets up the scenario that you purchase a $300,000 home in Raleigh, North Carolina, with a $60,000 down payment and an appreciation rate of 3 percent a year, and it concludes that "you'll end up with a decent, though not spectacular return of $117,300."

Right off the bat, I thought it was strange that the author used Raleigh as the example—at 3 percent appreciation per year. Raleigh is considered one of the hottest real estate markets in the country. After a short search, I found the actual appreciation in Raleigh since 2003, and the forecast through 2008, on the same magazine's Web site. Well, you can imagine my surprise when I found that over a five-year period between 2003 and 2008, the very same magazine (under another writer's byline) predicts that Raleigh will have, on average, 10.2 precent appreciation! Now that would make for a very different scenario, and one that wouldn't support the article's claim that this type of real estate investment will bring only a moderate return. Had the author used actual figures for the Raleigh market, the selling price would have been much closer to $487,561, not $358,200—nearly $130,000 more.

Now granted, not every market is going to appreciate at 10.2 percent every year—in fact most won't. As of this writing, the national average, however, for real estate appreciation is 6 percent. That is double the percentage used in the article's example. Applying a 6 percent appreciation rate, the house's selling price would have been $425,555—a full $67,355 more than the author's figure.

The other problem I had with the author's example is the way in which the return on the investment is calculated, which the author doesn't explain. Based on my experience after a long career in real estate investing, I question its accuracy. In real estate, and any other investment, your rate of return is based solely on the money you have in the deal. In this example, it would be figured by dividing the total return of $117,300 by the down payment, which was $60,000. The result is a 195.50 percent rate of return over the six years, or 32.58 percent per year—and that's just based on a 3 percent appreciation rate. That's the power of leverage, something we'll discuss in detail later in this section. I'll also show you why a real estate investment, at 6 percent appreciation (the national average at the time), will fare better than a stock at 10 percent. But for now let's look at the difference in rate of return between 3 percent appreciation and 6 percent appreciation using the article's scenario.

Since the 6 percent appreciation would have netted us an additional $67,355 over the article's 3 percent appreciation assumptions, we'll add that to the total return figure of $117,300 for an overall return of $184,655 over the six-year period. Divide that sum by the down payment of $60,000, and we have a rate of return of an astounding 307 percent, or 51 percent per year! If we did the same calculations based on the appreciation rate we found on the magazine's Web site, 10.2 percent, the rate of return would be substantially more! As you can see, if the author had used these more favorable figures, the article's conclusion would have been different.

Another important fact that the article doesn't address is that the interest payments in this scenario, $59,700, would be tax-deductible. Those savings are not factored into the return calculations. Nor do they include the rent of $1,700 per month (the author's figure) as income toward the property's operating expenses. Instead she makes a subtle shift by saying it is a savings to you of $14,700. One term is passive, the other active. A $14,700 savings would assume that it's money you don't have to pay out of pocket—meaning your existing salary. But actually, a $14,700 income from the property would be *over and above* your existing income streams. This distinction is not highlighted, but it makes a big difference in real life. The property's expenses are sustained by the property itself, not by you, and you get $14,700 in actual cash—not just savings—to boot. By doing so, the article omits one of the biggest advantages of owning investment real estate: cash flow.

The last and biggest issue I had with this article is that it's based on the buy-and-flip model. Many of the examples the author uses to contrast real estate investing with stocks factor in the gains from real estate investing over only a couple years. But this is a poor investment model. Indeed, the author is absolutely correct that if you invest in real estate in order to flip, your expenses will be higher and your returns lower. The transaction costs of commissions, closing costs, and so on, are just too high. But real estate generally is a long-term investment, and its benefits are best realized over the long term.

In the remainder of this chapter I'll show you ten reasons why real estate can often be the best investment over any other type out there.

#1. *Cash Flow*

First things first: I always purchase properties that cash-flow. It takes time to find them, but it is well worth the effort. The simplest definition of positive cash flow is that you collect more revenue, usually in the form of rent, than it takes to pay for and operate the property. A big advantage of real estate over other investments is that it can produce cash flow on a monthly basis. The cash generated by a real estate investment will always be a much larger percentage cash-on-cash return than any other investment. The reason for this is the leverage, something we'll go deeper into later in this chapter.

The beauty of a cash-flowing real estate property is that it can help you become financially free. Here is an exercise that I like to do when I speak at *Rich Dad* seminars. Take out a pen and a paper and write down your net monthly income after taxes and Social Security. Now, write down every expense that you have in a given month. It might look something like this:

Monthly Income		
Net income (salary)		**4,500**
Monthly Expenses		
Item		**Cost**
Mortgage		1,600
Insurance		200
Car Payment		500
Gas		180
Groceries		500
Utilities		300
Clothing		150
Entertainment		300
Total		**3,730**
Monthly Cash Flow	**$**	**770**

This is your cash flow statement. Your list will probably be more detailed than this. Make sure to write down everything that you really do spend in a month. Now take your hand and cover up the income portion of your cash flow statement. This is what your retirement could be like if you don't begin investing now—a whole stack of bills and nothing coming in to pay them.

In *Rich Dad, Poor Dad*, Robert Kiyosaki talks extensively about the need to understand your income statement. It is very simple. You have income and expenses, and assets and liabilities. In order to become wealthy you have to stop working just to pay your expenses and wasting the rest on liabilities. You need to begin buying assets.

Here is how most people's financial statements look. Money comes in the form of a paycheck each month. With that they pay their expenses. Then they purchase liabilities with the rest. It is money out the door and going into the pockets of the wealthy.

Rich Dad Cash Flow Scenario #1

Instead of purchasing liabilities you should be purchasing assets. Only then will you be able to build your wealth. Your financial statement should look like this:

Rich Dad Cash Flow Scenario #2

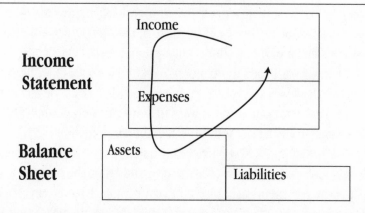

**Income
Statement**

**Balance
Sheet**

Do you see the difference? In the first example your money flows out of your hands into the hands of others because you are purchasing liabilities that depreciate in value. In the example above, however, you purchase assets and they in turn create more income.

Take our example income statement again.

Monthly Income		
Net income (salary)		**4,500**
Monthly Expenses		
Item		**Cost**
Mortgage		1,600
Insurance		200
Car Payment		500
Gas		180
Groceries		500
Utilities		300
Clothing		150
Entertainment		300
Total		**3,730**
Monthly Cash Flow	**$**	**770**

At the end of the month, after all the bills are paid, there is still $770 left. What would you do with an extra $770 per month? Right now it may be easy to say that you would invest it in assets like in the *Rich Dad* Cash Flow Scenario #2. It's much harder to do so once you have it burning a hole in your pocket. I know what I used to do. I used to spend it on liabilities like in Scenario #1. Maybe it was a new car, or a big screen TV. It could be any number of things to you. The point is that it went to items that only depreciated once I bought them. They did not grow in value; therefore neither did I.

If you are anything like I was before my financial education, there is a major realignment that needs to take place in your thought process when it comes to how you spend your discretionary income. That money would be much better spent by investing in assets. Especially income-producing assets like real estate. That $770 per month on the cash flow statement above equals out to $9,240 per year. With a little time and patience that money could easily be used as a down payment on a property that cash-flows. Buy enough properties that cash-flow and soon your expenses will be covered by those assets alone. Each and every month, cash flow from your investment properties will roll in. If you had to stop working, you would have the peace of mind to know that your investments could produce enough income on their own to cover your living expenses.

Financial freedom can mean any number of things to you. For me it's the freedom of choice. I'm not talking about a certain highly politicized issue here. I'm talking about the ability to control my life and my schedule. I don't answer to anyone—except my wife—when it comes to how I spend my time. There is no company or boss that tells me when I should be in the office. My time is my own. That frees me up to spend my time with my family and friends. Every summer I pack up and head to San Diego with my family. I spend three months away from the stifling heat of the Phoenix summers with my kids and my beautiful wife on a sunny California beach doing what I want and enjoying every moment of it. I can rest assured that my business will still be there when I get back. All the while it makes money for me while I play, and my wealth continues to grow. *That* is freedom to me.

That is something stocks and other investments can't do for you. While returns may be good if you invest correctly in stocks, bonds, and mutual funds, those investments produce liquidity that has to be reinvested or is taxed as ordinary income. It is true that you may receive a quarterly dividend, but that won't be enough to cover even a portion of your living expenses. Effectively, your money is tied up while corporations use it to make even more money. If you need to get some cash, you have to sell some stock and then it's taxed.

#2. Control

A unique advantage to real estate is that you can control it. In other types of investments, you give your money to a financial advisor and they place it for you in a company's stock, a bond, or a mutual fund. What happens after that is completely out of your control. You have no ability to make operating decisions for the company you have invested in; you are at the mercy of its managers. One bad decision having nothing to do with you can totally ruin your portfolio—just ask the people whose entire retirement was dependent on Enron. Similarly, you have no control over financial markets when you purchase bonds or futures. You make a calculated guess, and then you sit back and watch. With these types of investments, the only control you have is choosing whether to buy or to sell.

Real estate is different. You purchase a tangible asset and you manage it. While it is true that there are still external market conditions that affect your investment, the difference is that you have the ability to manipulate the operations of your investment to respond to those conditions. Instead of being reactive (buying or selling), you are being proactive.

For example, if you are a landlord, you have the ability to manipulate rents based on changing market conditions in order to maximize income. I do this all the time in my company—both with properties that I own and properties that I manage for others. Each month my managers are required to do a market survey. A market survey is a simple study that involves calling your direct competitors and asking them what they are charging for rents, deposits, and what they are offering for concessions, if anything. By gathering this data, my managers are able to make real-time market decisions by comparing their rents, deposits, and concessions—again, if any—against their competitors and adjusting accordingly.

This doesn't always mean raising rents either. Again, the goal is to maximize income. Since that is a dynamic process, that might mean lowering rents or offering an incentive. The property's occupancy comes into play here. If you have the highest rents in a market, chances are potential residents will go down the road and rent from a direct competitor. Then all your high rents become lost potential income. The dynamics of real estate require you to keep occupancy, as well as rents, high. If lowering rents by $15 per month is the difference between being 95 percent occupied or being 88 percent occupied, then by all means lower your rents! Here is a simple chart to show you why:

100-Unit Building

Average Rents	Occupancy	Total Rental Income
$ 685	95%	$ 65,075
$ 700	88%	$ 61,600

Per this example, just by lowering your rent by $15 per month on average, you actually gain close to $3,500 per month in income—that's nearly $42,000 per year. Lowering rents gradually can lead to higher occupancy. Based on a 6 percent capitalization rate, that is $700,000 ($42,000 ÷ 6 percent) in value, all because you were on top of the market and able to make a real-time, proactive decision. You have the power in real estate to control the operational performance of your asset more than any other investment. As I explained in my book, *The ABC's of Real Estate Investing,* the capitalization rate is the net operating income divided by the purchase price, and is determined by evaluating recent sales statistics of similar properties in a given market. Your broker will be a valuable tool in determining your market's capitalization rate.

Capitalization Rate = Net Operating Income ÷ Purchase Price

#3. Appreciation

When it comes to appreciation, the old adage is true: location, location, location. Did you know that since 1968, historic appreciation levels for real estate have been 6 percent per year, according to the National Association of Realtors? The graph speaks for itself. The graph accounts for the entire nation. That means there are areas that perform poorly and areas that are rock stars. So, if the average is 6 percent, then there are areas that have lower appreciation rates and areas that have higher ones. In the next section I'll show you why even at 6 percent you are realizing far better returns on your money than a stock that returns 15 percent, but for now let's focus on appreciation for appreciation's sake.

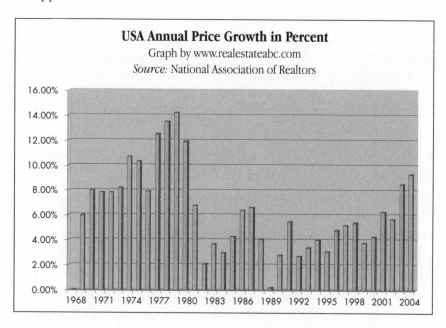

If you are purchasing a property that cash-flows, appreciation is just icing on the cake. By doing a little bit of homework you can find areas that will have appreciation levels far above the national average. These areas will be places like Phoenix, Seattle, Boise, New York City, and Washington, D.C., where the job growth and employment growth are high. Cash flow coupled with appreciation is a very potent combination. Let's explore an example of this. Assume you are purchasing a $200,000 property at 20 percent down ($40,000) and that rents for $1,000 per month. Where do you think that investment will be in thirty years? Take a look at the chart.

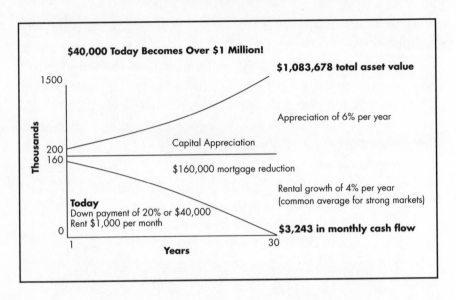

Here is what is so exciting about investment real estate: Over time, your property is appreciating while the resident is paying down your loan. On top of this, the rental income also grows on a percentage annual basis!

In the example, you can see how a relatively small real estate investment over time becomes a powerful part of your retirement. After thirty years, the average life of a mortgage, the property is worth $1,083,678. Not only is the property paid off and worth an incredible $883,678 more than when you purchased it, but the rental income also comes in every month with very little effort on your part. It's cash flow that comes into your account while you are sleeping, playing, and experiencing life. While the mortgage was being paid off, the rental income was growing at 4 percent per year and is now providing you with $3,243 per month. That is $38,916 in annual income from just one property.

Real estate is always better as a long-term investment because of the appreciation and cash flow advantages.

As I mentioned earlier, I'm not a fan of flipping a property for profit. Those that flip properties are almost no better off than those who invest in stock markets. By doing so, you always have to search for a new place to put your money or else you will be hit with a huge tax bill because of the tax on capital gains. What makes the example above work is the principle of buy-and-hold. If you must sell, you should at least keep the property more than two years after you acquire it because your capital gains tax liability is lower.

The most beautiful thing about this example is that you only put $40,000 down when you purchased the $200,000 investment. By using the bank's money, your money realized a much higher return than if you had invested it in stocks or bonds. That is called leverage, and leverage is the ultimate power of real estate. Appreciation grows on the "loaned" amount. So the $160,000 at 6 percent per year over thirty years with the magic of compounding grows to a value of $918,959! You get that money, not the bank. All they receive is the interest on the original loan, and you can even write off the interest expense come tax time.

#4. *Leverage and Other People's Money (OPM)*

Leverage is my favorite thing about investing in real estate. I think you will feel the same way after you read this section. It's more than likely you have heard the term Other People's Money, or OPM, tossed around. You may have even read the book written by Michael Lechter in the *Rich Dad* series, *OPM: Other People's Money*. The concept is simple and powerful.

The OPM concept is using money generated from someone or something other than you in order to start a business or acquire an asset. While it is true that you can do this to an extent with stocks through buying on margin, the fact is that there is no investment where the application of this tool is more powerful than in real estate. In real estate the leverage is based on the *asset itself* and you can get a bank to loan you the money up to 80 percent, and sometimes even 90 to 100 percent, of the total asset value. Why do banks do this? Because they can repossess the physical asset itself should you default. Buying stocks on margin, however, allows you to borrow no more than 50 percent of the stock portfolio value. Just try to get a bank to loan you the money for buying stocks—let alone your margin! Instead, you have to buy through a brokerage—at a high interest rate. In other words, when you buy stocks on margin, you are taking the risk. But when you take out a loan to buy real estate, the bank is assuming the risk.

What is more, buying on margin is riskier because of the volatility of the market. If your portfolio takes a huge dip, you still have to pay the margin, but have no asset to fall back on. Buying on margin is an investment where you can actually stand to lose more money than you invested. In real estate, you have the physical asset itself to fall back on, and it is a slow-moving investment so the asset has less volatility, which is why a bank will be your partner. As we learned earlier, the national average for real estate appreciation is 6 percent, and leverage is the ultimate wealth-generator when it comes to taking advantage of that appreciation.

So how is it that an investment in real estate at a 6 percent appreciation rate is by far a better investment than a stock at 10 percent? One word: leverage. When you leverage an investment, you reap the benefits of the appreciation on the total asset value, while only having a small percentage of your own money in the deal. Using the same example that we used earlier in the chapter, I'll show you how this works.

In any investment, the goal is to have the highest cash-on-cash return, or return on investment (ROI) possible. ROI is the percentage return of your investment to your invested dollars. In order to determine ROI, you divide the amount earned by the original investment.

ROI = Return on investment ÷ Original investment

Let's take the equation from above and apply it to our $200,000 property. Given the fact that after thirty years the property is worth $1,083,678, that means to find our profit, we'll divide that number by our $40,000 original cash investment to find our percentage ROI.

$1,083,678 ÷ $40,000 = 2,709% ÷ 30 years = 90.3% per year

Our ROI would be 90 percent. How unbelievable is that? And that *doesn't even include* the cash flow generated from the property or your tax breaks! You've probably checked my math a couple of times after looking at that percentage return! Now let's compare that return on a $40,000 down payment on a $200,000 property at 6 percent appreciation to a $40,000 investment in stock at 10 percent per year for the same amount of time.

If you held on to your stock for thirty years, and *if* the stock appreciated at 10 percent per year for thirty years, your $40,000 of stock would be worth $634,524. That would mean your ROI would be:

$634,524 ÷ $40,000 = 1,586 percent ÷ 30 years = 52.8 percent per year

Don't get me wrong, 1,658 percent return on your money is an awesome return. But it isn't the best return you could have. Isn't it amazing that a return on a stock that produces 10 percent per year is nearly 50 percent less than a property that only grows at 6 percent per year? That doesn't even take into account the fact that you could have tax-free cash flow from real estate and

$40,000 Down / $200,000 Investment			
Year	Appreciation at 6%	Appreciation at 8%	Appreciation at 10%
1	$ —	$ —	$ —
2	$ 12,000	$ 16,000	$ 20,000
3	$ 24,720	$ 33,280	$ 42,000
4	$ 38,203	$ 51,942	$ 66,200
5	$ 52,495	$ 72,098	$ 92,820
6	$ 67,645	$ 93,866	$ 122,102
7	$ 83,704	$ 117,375	$ 154,312
8	$ 100,726	$ 142,765	$ 189,743
9	$ 118,770	$ 170,186	$ 228,718
10	$ 137,896	$ 199,801	$ 271,590
11	$ 158,170	$ 231,785	$ 318,748
12	$ 179,660	$ 266,328	$ 370,623
13	$ 202,439	$ 303,634	$ 427,686
14	$ 226,586	$ 343,925	$ 490,454
15	$ 252,181	$ 387,439	$ 559,500
16	$ 279,312	$ 434,434	$ 635,450
17	$ 308,070	$ 485,189	$ 718,995
18	$ 338,555	$ 540,004	$ 810,894
19	$ 370,868	$ 599,204	$ 911,983
20	$ 405,120	$ 663,140	$ 1,023,182
21	$ 441,427	$ 732,191	$ 1,145,500
22	$ 479,913	$ 806,767	$ 1,280,050
23	$ 520,707	$ 887,308	$ 1,428,055
24	$ 563,950	$ 974,293	$ 1,590,860
25	$ 609,787	$ 1,068,236	$ 1,769,947
26	$ 658,374	$ 1,169,695	$ 1,966,941
27	$ 709,877	$ 1,279,271	$ 2,183,635
28	$ 764,469	$ 1,397,612	$ 2,421,999
29	$ 822,337	$ 1,525,421	$ 2,684,199
30	$ 883,678	$ 1,663,455	$ 2,972,619
ROI	**$883,678**	**$1,663,455**	**$2,972,619**

that you cannot get from a stock or a bond. That is the magic of leverage, and the power of real estate. And 6 percent is simply the national *average* for appreciation. If you do your homework, more times than not, you will find markets and purchase property where the appreciation level is well above the national average of 6 percent. I've prepared a chart on the previous page that details how astonishing returns on a solid real estate investment can really be in markets that appreciate at higher than the national average.

I know that's a lot of numbers, but that's some pretty unbelievable appreciation. Now let's quickly look at an apple-for-apple comparison of the returns from a leveraged investment like real estate versus the returns from an unleveraged investment, like a stock or bond, at the same rate of growth over thirty years. With a leveraged investment, the same dollar amount invested in real estate will net you many times more than in an unleveraged investment based on the same returns. That is just based on pure appreciation. There are a variety of tax advantages to the real estate investment over a stock or a bond as well.

Stocks vs. Real Estate over 30 Years									
Appreciation	Amount	Real Estate Value	Rate of Return	Growth	Stocks	Rate of Return	% Difference	per year
6%	$40,000	$1,083,678	2709%	6%	$216,736	542%	2167%	72%
8%	$40,000	$1,863,455	4659%	8%	$372,691	932%	3727%	124%
10%	$40,000	$3,172,619	7932%	10%	$634,524	1586%	6345%	212%

#5. Depreciation

The IRS considers depreciation to be an income tax deduction that allows a taxpayer to recover the cost or other basis of certain property. It is an annual allowance for wear and tear, deterioration, or obsolescence of the property.

For the purposes of real estate investment, it's a nonoperational expense that can be used to your advantage come tax time. There are different classes of depreciation. The IRS will allow you to calculate your depreciation expense based on tables they provide, showing you the number of years that you can depreciate a property. The depreciable years are vastly different depending on the asset. For instance, residential investment real estate is 27.5 years, while commercial real estate is 39 years.

The basic equation for figuring depreciation is:

(Total Asset Value — Land Value) ÷ Depreciable Years = Annual Depreciation

For example, my partner, Ross, our investors, and I recently acquired a building in Flagstaff, Arizona. The total value of the asset was $19.7 million. In order to estimate our depreciation, we have to first subtract the value of the land, since the IRS doesn't consider that to be a depreciable asset. Depreciation only accounts for the buildings on the land, since they will lose value as they age. The estimated value of the land is $3 million. Now let's calculate our yearly depreciation based on the IRS table of 27.5 years. (Don't ask me why they use that number. I certainly can't explain the mysteries of the Internal Revenue Service.)

$$(\$19,700,000 - \$3,000,000) \div 27.5 \text{ years} = \$607,273$$

Now I'll show you why this is so important. Remember that depreciation is treated as a nonoperational expense. Therefore I can use that $607,273 per year against my cash flow when the tax man comes rolling around. Here is a simple chart to show you why depreciation is so powerful.

Purchase Price	$19,700,000
Land Value	$ 3,000,000
Total Depreciable Value	$16,700,000
Yearly Depreciation	$ (607,273)

Now look at how that applies to a simplified property financial:

Rental Income	$ 2,200,000
Other Income	$ 500,000
Total Income	$ 2,700,000
Operating Expenses	$ 1,500,000
Net Operating Income	$ 1,200,000
Debt Service	$ 900,000
Cash Flow	$ 300,000
Depreciation	$ (607,273)
Net Income after Depreciation	$ (307,273)

What you see reflected in the chart is what I like to refer to as tax-free cash flow. The cash flow for the property after all operational expenses is $300,000. That would warrant a pretty hefty tax bill come April, but depreciation allows me to show an operating *loss* of $307,273. That means in reality since the depreciation is a noncash expense *I don't have to pay any taxes,* even though my investors and I have pocketed $300,000. And I can use the tax savings for other investments. Thanks, IRS!

One word of caution: recapture. If you sell your property, the IRS rules require you to recapture the money that you have depreciated. Thankfully, there are ways around recapture, such as a 1031 exchange, something we'll explore in detail later on. But for now, it suffices to say that the tax advantages of depreciation are an incredible investment tool.

Money tends to produce more money—when invested right. With our property producing $300,000 per year in tax-free cash flow, we are able to roll that into other leveraged investments. Each time we take advantage of our leveraged return on our money and our tax-free cash flow, thanks to the IRS rules, this allows us to steadily compound our wealth at an exponential rate that is impossible to do with standard investments.

#6. Refinance

Another advantage of real estate over other investments is the ability to withdraw cash through a refinance of the property. This, too, is a tax-free transaction. When you refinance a property you are restructuring your existing mortgage debt based on the added value of the property.

In almost every instance, I will opt to refinance a property rather than sell it. In fact, I did this just recently with two of the properties in my company's portfolio. One of the properties is a senior housing property, located in Sun City, Arizona, that we purchased for $9 million from an investor who lived out of state and we obtained a loan for $7.2 million. We knew that we could improve the operations on the property by adding first-floor premiums of $50 per month (many seniors prefer first-floor over second-floor units), and we added amenities to create higher occupancy such as a 26-passenger shuttle bus. In the first year alone, our improvements to operations increased the value of the property by $910,000.

In acquiring the building, we employed our usual acquisition plan, which is to raise all the equity for the down payment from our investors. Almost immediately our investors were realizing very strong rates of return because our improvements to operations created substantial cash flow. The business plan was to refinance after a number of years, and we did just that.

Five years later the property appraised at $15 million, and we refinanced it (two years ahead of schedule) for $12.26 million. That is a tax-free gain of nearly $5 million and over $1 million per year—just from improvements to operations and sound management. From the refinance, I was able to pay back all the original equity that I collected, plus a percentage return on the equity to the investors, plus my partner and I pocketed over $1 million for ourselves. Not bad. Now my investors have all their original money back, and they continue to get cash flow from the property. My investors are happy, and we're happy. The property's operations more than cover the higher mortgage payment, and, best of all, the money from the refinance is tax-free. Our investment is now zero, and our return is . . . infinite!

#7. *Asset Protection*

There are a number of ways to legally protect your real estate investment that cannot be utilized with other standard investments. With stocks and bonds, for instance, if the company you are invested in has a bad year, you are simply out of luck.

Though insurance is a big cost in real estate investments, it's generally covered by the property's income. Thus, it is essentially free to you since it is an operation cost to the property. Oh, by the way, it is a tax-deductible expense.

You are, of course, familiar with insurance. It's one of life's necessities that go beyond the realm of real estate investing. But most people don't ever think about the fact that real estate is one of the few investments that can be insured. When you invest in real estate, you have peace of mind knowing that if the real property is destroyed for whatever reason, and you have the proper insurance coverage, you are able to claim your losses for the actual value of the asset *before* the loss, and *during* the loss.

Another distinct legal advantage of real estate is that it can be placed into a limited liability company, or an LLC. Garrett Sutton, an advisor to the *Rich Dad* team, and I have written fairly extensively on this topic. An LLC allows you to protect your personal wealth by individualizing and protecting your assets. If, for any reason, you were to be sued, your other personal assets like your house, bank accounts, and investments would be protected because they wouldn't be property of your LLC.

Each and every property that you buy should be placed in its own individual LLC. That is one of the greatest ways to protect your wealth. Imagine you own multiple investment properties and one of your residents fell in the shower and became injured. If all of your properties were under a single entity, that resident would have the legal right to pursue damages based on the entire asset value of all your investments in that entity. If, however, each property was its own legal entity through an LLC, that resident should only be able to seek damages from that entity. Your other holdings would not be affected.

In addition to the legal protections that an LLC provides, there are also distinct tax advantages. For example, one of my companies, MC Management, is an LLC and handles all property management services for all of our investments. My vehicle and all of its expenses, and my travel expenses to find new deals, are all paid from this company. In other words, most of my expenses are "company expenses." Most people pay their car payments, gas, insurance, and so on after the traditional taxes are taken out of their paycheck. You have to be careful here. Your LLC needs to have legitimate business activities and you need to be able to show that your company expenses are valid. You should always check with an accountant and a legal advisor when structuring your LLCs. For more information on tax and legal structures, I recommend you read *Real Estate Advantages* by Sharon Lechter and Garrett Sutton.

#8. 1031 Exchanges

My friend and business colleague Gary Gorman is an expert in 1031 exchanges. He has over thirty-five years' experience in real estate tax transactions, and is the author of the book *Exchanging Up*. I'm not a 1031 expert, so I sought Gary out when I was looking for education on the subject. He has been an invaluable asset to me as part of my investment team and is well known to Robert Kiyosaki and the *Rich Dad* team as an expert when it comes to 1031 exchanges.

I asked Gary to help me on this section of my book, and all the wise advice on 1031 exchanges in this book is a direct result of Gary's input.

So you've bought your apartment building, solved its problems, fixed it up, and now it's worth a whole lot more than you paid for it. Now what? That's easy—you sell it, buy another building, and do it again! But let's think this through. If you sell the old building outright, you'll pay tax on the sale, which will reduce the proceeds available for the purchase of the new property. A reduction in available funds will reduce the amount of new property you can buy, which will reduce future appreciation.

For example, let's assume that the tax on the gain from your sale is $1 million, and assume also that the bank will make you a 75 percent loan. In other words, for every one dollar you put up, the bank will lend you three. This means that if there were a way you could avoid paying the tax of $1 million right now, you'd be able to borrow an additional $3 million from the bank, which means that you could buy a property for $4 million more than you'd be able to afford if you had to pay the tax.

So, is there a way to avoid, or at least defer, paying tax on the sale of your old property? Yes, and that way is through a 1031 exchange. Section 1031 of the Internal Revenue Code provides that the gain from the sale rolls over from your old property to your new, if you follow certain rules. Although the law is called a 1031 "exchange," you are not really swapping the deed of your property for the deed of the property you want. In actuality, you sell your old property and then, within a certain period of time, purchase the replacement property you've chosen.

A 1031 exchange is available only for property held for investment or used in a trade or business. A 1031 exchange does not apply to your personal residence, meaning the house you live in. You can exchange any type of investment property for any other type of investment property. For example, if you sell a duplex, you can buy any other type of investment property. You could buy an office building, or an apartment building, a warehouse, or even bare land. Or you could sell bare land and buy income-producing property in order to increase cash flow, which is a popular investment strategy.

Section 1031 does not allow you to do an exchange on property you hold for "resale," although the IRS does not define that term. Essentially it means property that you buy with the intent of immediately selling it rather than holding it for investment. A classic example of property held for resale is the "fix-and-flip." A fix-and-flip is where you buy a distressed property with the intent to quickly fix it up and then sell it. The commonly accepted rule of thumb is that the difference between property held for investment (which qualifies for an exchange), and property held for resale (which doesn't), is *a year and a day*. Generally speaking, if you hold both your old property and your new property for at least a year and a day (each), you've met the investment property requirement.

Certainly the scariest part of doing a 1031 exchange for most people is the requirement that you not touch the money in between the sale of your old property and the purchase of your new. By law the money from the sale has to be held by an independent third party called a "qualified intermediary." Intermediaries have two primary roles: They prepare the exchange documents that are required by Section 1031, and they hold the money during the exchange.

The problem is that almost anyone can be an intermediary. Certain people are excluded from being an intermediary (people like your attorney, your CPA, or anyone that is related to you), but essentially anyone else can be an intermediary. And this creates potential problems for you and your exchange. The problem is that they must hold your money after the sale of your old property until the purchase of your new. Since virtually anyone could be an intermediary, there is really no reason why a convicted felon couldn't be your intermediary and hold your money. And yes, convicted felons have entered the intermediary business, so make sure you know who you are dealing with.

Related to this is the fact that most intermediaries hold their client's money in a commingled, or pooled, account. This means that they hold everyone's money in the same account. This is tremendously risky for you because there is a court case that has ruled that such an account is available to any creditor of the intermediary. If one of the intermediary's employees is on their way to the bank on intermediary business and they hit a school bus, the parents could sue the intermediary and get your money.

Commingled accounts are also tempting to less scrupulous intermediaries. Over the years several very large intermediaries have suddenly gone out of business resulting in the loss of many millions of dollars.

Courts have stated a number of times that money held in a separate account by an intermediary is protected from the intermediary's creditors. So you *must* insist that your intermediary hold your money in a separate account just for you. This is critical. Do not let your intermediary commingle your money with anyone else's. And make sure that your name is identified with the account, and make sure that your tax identification number is also associated with the account so that there is no possibility for confusion about who the money is being held for.

It is virtually impossible to tell whether the intermediary you're working with is trustworthy or not. It doesn't matter how experienced they are, or how big the company is, so the only surefire way of protecting yourself is to make sure the money is held in a separate account. There is no state or federal government agency watching out for you—you are entirely on your own. It's your money, and in the end no one but you is responsible for its safety.

Once you've closed the sale, as the seller of your investment real estate, a couple of time limits are imposed by Section 1031. The first of these time frames is the requirement that from the day you close your investment real estate you have exactly forty-five days to make a list of properties you might want to buy. You typically want three properties or fewer on this list. This is because there are no limits on your list if it has three properties or fewer.

If you put more than three properties on your list, you become subject to the "200 percent rule" of Section 1031, which says that, since your list is more than three (whether it has four, or ten, or forty properties), the total combined purchase price of everything on the list cannot be more than twice the selling price of your old property.

Let's say that you sell your apartment building for $1 million and you list three properties worth $10 million each, for a total of $30 million. Is this okay? Yes—because your list only had three properties on it. But what if your list shows four properties for only $750,000 each—is this okay? No, since your list has more than three properties on it, you can only list $2 million worth of properties (twice the $1 million selling price of your apartment building). Since four times $750,000 is $3 million, which exceeds your 200 percent limit, your exchange is in jeopardy. And your whole exchange is taxable even if you bought one of the properties. So, be smart—keep it simple by keeping your list to three properties or fewer.

How do you complete your list? You have to list each property in terms that are clear enough that an IRS agent could take your list and go directly to the door of the property. This means, for example, that if one of your properties happens to be in the Phoenix Condominium Towers, you have to list Unit 203—you can't simply say 123 Camelback Road (the address of the towers). Once you've completed your list, give it to your qualified intermediary. Just make sure that it is in your intermediary's hands before midnight on the forty-fifth day.

The second time limit rule states that from the day you close the sale of your investment real estate, you have exactly 180 days in which to buy your replacement property, and whatever you buy has to be on the forty-five day list. This means that you can buy one, two, or all three of the properties on your list. Just make sure that you actually close the purchase, because "closing in escrow" or doing a "dry closing" does not meet the requirements; title to the new property has to be in your name before midnight of the 180th day.

And like the forty-five-day requirement, these are calendar days, and there are no extensions—if the 180th day falls on a Saturday, or Sunday, or a holiday (like the Fourth of July), then that is the day. One exception to this requirement that you have to be careful of is that if your 180th day falls after the due date of your tax return (such as April 15), and you have not purchased your replacement property, you will need to extend your tax return. This is because if you file your tax return without reporting your exchange, then your exchange is in jeopardy. And obviously you cannot properly report your exchange if you haven't purchased your new property.

In simple terms, you must take title to your new property the same way you held title to your old property. This means that you have to report them on the same tax return—using the same tax identification number or Social Security number.

Section 1031 applies to the taxpayer that owns the old property. This means that you have to take title to the new property in the same manner (in other words the same tax return) as the entity that owned the old property. For example, if Fred and Sue hold title to their apartment building in their own names (Fred and Sue Jones, for example), they cannot take title to the new property in the name of their corporation (Jones Investment Corporation) because the corporation files a tax return and is therefore a different taxpayer.

There are several exceptions to this rule dealing with what the IRS calls "disregarded entities," which are things like revocable living trusts and single-member limited liability companies. The discussion of disregarded entities is beyond the scope of this book, so if you would like to know more about this subject, you can get more information from Gary Gorman's Web site at www.expert1031.com, or ask your qualified intermediary to explain it to you. A good intermediary should be able to do so.

Just because you've sold your investment real estate and have contacted a qualified intermediary does not automatically mean that all the gain rolls from the sale of the old property into your new property. There are two additional things you must do in order to pay no tax: First, you must *buy equal or up*. If Fred and Sue sell their apartment building for $1 million, they must buy their new property for at least $1 million in order to owe no tax. If they buy down and only pay $900,000 for their new property, it doesn't mean that their exchange is in jeopardy—they simply pay tax on the $100,000 buy-down. And in a 1031 exchange the entire $100,000 buy-down would be taxable.

The second thing you have to do is *reinvest all of the cash* from the sale of the apartment building into the new property. If there was $400,000 of debt and closing costs when Fred and Sue sold their building, their intermediary will receive the balance of $600,000, and they must reinvest all that money in the new property in order to avoid paying tax on the sale. This is true even if they originally put $50,000 of their own cash into the purchase of the original investment real estate.

If Fred and Sue are buying their new building for $1.5 million, they do not have an equal-or-up problem since they sold for $1 million and are buying for $1.5 million. However, if they get a new loan for $1 million (which means that they only need $500,000 of the $600,000 that the intermediary is holding), they will pay tax on the leftover cash of $100,000 because they did not reinvest all of it. And, as I explained above, the entire $100,000 would be taxable. One thing that Fred and Sue could do to avoid this problem would be to reduce their loan to $900,000 so that they use the entire balance of $600,000 held by the intermediary.

Another way that Fred and Sue could have avoided paying tax in both of the examples above would be to buy a second property that would get them to their required equal-or-up computation and use any unspent cash. The second property would have to be on their forty-five-day list, of course.

One last thing I want to point out is that, contrary to the belief of most tax advisors, there is no requirement that the debt on the new property be equal or greater than the amount of debt on the old property. You only need to buy equal or up and reinvest all of the cash to avoid having to pay any tax. Many tax professionals, as well as most exchange advisors, are confused about this, but it's true—there is no debt replacement requirement.

What happens to the gain that gets rolled over? This is a common question, and the answer most people want to hear is that it disappears, but it doesn't. Your rollover gains are aggregated until you finally sell your last property and don't do a 1031 exchange. For example, if Fred and Sue roll over a $300,000 profit on the sale of the apartment building, and buy their replacement property for $1.5 million, they have a $300,000 built-in gain on that property. If they then sell that property for $2 million and decide not to do an exchange, their taxable gain will be $800,000 ($300,000 from the first property and $500,000 from the second). In the real world their gain will actually be greater than this because of something called depreciation recapture, but you get the idea. If Fred and Sue decided to do an exchange on the second property, their built-in gain on the third property would be $800,000, and they'd go on from there.

#9. Hedge Against Inflation

Many people feel that the commonsense thing to do is to take your money and put it into a savings bond or bank account that yields 2 to 3 percent per year. The main argument for this type of investing is that it is "safer" than real estate or other types of investments. The problem is that you don't make any money. The reason for this is inflation.

Inflation is the price of goods like cars, food, clothes, and so forth measured against a standard of ability to purchase those goods. For instance, gas prices have been rising pretty heavily lately. I don't know about you, but in my area I've seen them rise from $2 to over $3 in just over a year. That is a 50 percent increase! Now, there is no way that salaries are rising at the same rate. That means I have less purchasing power when it comes to gas than I did a year ago because my money doesn't buy me as much as it used to.

Gas is a pretty extreme example, but the fact remains that the price for consumer goods rises, and at a pretty good rate. According to InflationData.com, the long-term average of inflation has been nearly 3.5 percent since 1913, the year it began being tracked. That means that putting money into a bank investment or account that yields only 2 to 3 percent earns you no purchasing power in the future. You are actually losing wealth because inflation is higher than your returns. The gain in interest is wiped out by the rising cost of living. You are not becoming wealthier, you are just maintaining.

Another important fact is that the only time inflation was negative over the last century was during the Great Depression. If you factor that out, inflation has been 4.1 percent historically. That means that if you have your money in a savings account that yields 3 percent per year, you are actually becoming poorer because the cost of goods is growing faster than the value of your money.

The beauty of real estate is that it is a tangible asset—a good. That means that it will generally rise either at the rate of inflation or much higher. In fact, some of the items that make up inflation are composed of real estate. That is proven by the statistic I used earlier in this section. Historically real estate has risen at 6 percent per year—a full 2 to 3 percent higher than inflation. And that is just appreciation. That doesn't take into account the cash flow generated from a real estate investment. Nor does it include the tax advantages of what I call the triple threat: refinancing, depreciation, and tax-deductible mortgage interest.

> **A big advantage of real estate over other investments is the triple threat of tax advantages: refinancing, depreciation, and tax-deductible mortgage interest.**

So, while many may think of real estate as an "unsafe" investment, they are not thinking through the implications of low-yield "safe" investments. Oftentimes, even real estate investments that perform poorly will still perform better than a "safe" investment, given inflation. What "safe" really means to the financially uneducated is guaranteed. In reality, though, the only guarantee of a guaranteed investment is that it will barely outpace inflation, if at all. All the while, the financially savvy banks that are using your money will be investing in "unsafe" investments, hedging against inflation and experiencing huge returns.

#10. *Let's Get Physical*

Real estate is a physical asset. It's not some cerebral investment that is traded by the click of a button on an online brokerage. I can hop into my car and drive to any one of my properties. I can walk the grounds, inspect the buildings, and question my staff. As such, it's not subject to the volatility of other investments like stocks.

With other types of investments, change can happen fast. For instance, when it comes to stocks, you are at the mercy of the company's public relations department. You wait to hear from them. That means that if the company announces poor earnings for a quarter, the stock will drop fast and with little warning. Again, all you can do is react, but not before you've lost a substantial sum.

Real estate is different. While it still has its ups and downs, for the most part, real estate takes a more tortoiselike approach: Slow and steady wins the race. If you are paying attention and know what to look for, you can see the trends that lead to changes in the real estate market well before they happen. This allows you to formulate an investment plan on how to change your operations or to sell. Maximizing ROI, or cash-on-cash return, is the key.

Additionally, real estate is not as liquid as other investments. That means that it is not a quick buy-and-sell transaction. When you sell liquid investments, you earn cash that has to be taxed at a very high capital gains rate. As I've shown you in this section, with real estate, the gains are over the long term and there are a number of ways to avoid or defer tax exposure that give it a significant advantage over other investments.

Slow and Steady Wins the Race

Real estate markets are not nearly as volatile as other markets that rise and fall on a minute-by-minute basis. A distinct advantage to the real estate market is that because of its measured fluctuations it cannot be manipulated by programmed buying and selling. In many large investment firms, traded investments are managed by computers that are preprogrammed to buy or sell based on predetermined percentages. If a stock reaches a certain growth rate, the computer buys. If it drops to a certain percentage, the computer sells. This has been known to create some pretty wild swings in the stock market, and it has nothing to do with you or your fund manager. The computer creates the demand or the lack thereof through a nanosecond decision. If you own stock in a company through a mutual fund or a fund managed by your broker, your stocks are bought and sold without your knowledge—often through programmed buying-and selling.

The reason firms are able to do this with your investments is because, one, you have given them the authority to manage your own wealth for you, and two, they hold the certificates in their hands. In real estate, you have the physical title. If you want, you can even frame it and put it on your wall—though you might get some funny looks. But the point is you could if you wanted to. It is impossible for programmed buying and selling to happen in a real estate market because the transactional process is long and slow. You have to find a seller, allow for physical inspections, get loan documents, and sign them. There are no split-second decisions in real estate. Everything is slow and measured. And that's the way it should be.

The Power of Real Estate

In this chapter we've explored all the incredible advantages of real estate over any other type of investment. I firmly believe that there is nothing more powerful than real estate—it can change your life.

As people live longer, the monetary needs for a comfortable retirement are much greater. As evidenced by this chapter, there are very few investments—if any at all—that can match the wealth-building power of real estate. If you purchased correctly, when you are ready to retire, your investment properties will be there waiting for you. Their mortgages will have been paid off either entirely or substantially by your residents, the value of the land will have grown by leaps and bounds, and the property will be generating monthly cash flow income for you so that you can enjoy your retirement without income worries.

Having established the power of real estate as an investment, I'm now going to shift focus to the main topic of this book, which is multifamily investing. In the next chapter I'll show you why an investment in apartments is the smartest real estate investment out there, and then I'll show you how you can purchase your own apartment building and be on your way toward changing your life forever.

Chapter 2

Why Multifamily? Apartment Power

One indicator that real estate outperforms any other investment is the performance of real estate investment trusts, or REITs as they are commonly called. REITs are publicly traded large portfolios of real estate that are open for investment. REITs are required by the government to distribute 90 percent of their profits to their investors in exchange for little or no corporate income tax.

According to the National Association of Real Estate Investment Trusts, REITs have outperformed every U.S. benchmark over the last thirty years.

Here are the compounded annual returns of REITs versus the U.S. benchmarks from 1975 to 2005:

Benchmark	Return
Dow Jones Industrial Average	8.8%
NASDAQ Composite	10.9%
S&P 500	12.7%
REITs	13.8%

This is, of course, just more proof of the primacy of real estate over other investments. The numbers are public statistics; they don't even include depreciation or other tax advantages, but they still trump traditional investing methods. A closer look at REITs reveals that apartment REITs continually outperform any other type of REIT investment. They are the crème de la crème of the real estate investment world.

In September 2006, the *New York Times* published an article entitled "It's a Good Time to Be a Landlord." According to the article, apartment REITs outperformed all other REIT sectors with total returns of 34.4 percent versus 23.3 percent. What is more, ten of the top twenty-five performing REITs were comprised of multifamily investments. What accounts for the primacy of multifamily investments over other real estate investment types? In this chapter I'll outline the five reasons multifamily properties are the ultimate real estate investment.

#1. Cash Flow

In the previous chapter I showed you why cash flow is such a vital element of the power of real estate investments. If you don't have a property management company on your investment team—get one now. Properties that are managed well are properties that realize net operating income growth every year. This takes expertise and a lot of time. Unless you are an expert in property management, there is no way you can ratchet up a property's performance like a professional property management company can. I've managed properties that annually grew in value at a $1 million clip simply by executing a sound management plan and increasing the net operating income. The basic principle behind sound property management is reduction of expenses and increase in income. Sounds simple, but it takes real expertise to do this.

Like a lot of real estate investments, apartment cash flow provides you with passive income that can be tax-free after depreciation. The distinct advantage that apartments have over other types of real estate like commercial is that cash flow can be manipulated quickly.

In commercial real estate leases can be for many years. If I'm the landlord, that is a scary proposition. While the security of a long-term lease is nice, it doesn't allow you to take advantage of fluctuations in the market. For instance, imagine you own a piece of commercial office space and sign a lease with a resident at the going rate of $4,000 per month for three years. One year later, demand increases and the going rate is now $4,500 per month. Because you have signed a long-term lease, you cannot take advantage of this upswing. Essentially you would be leaving at a minimum $500 per month on the table every year. That works out to $12,000 in lost income from just one commercial space.

In multifamily investments leases tend to last normally six to twelve months. This allows for constant adjustment of rents—up or down, if necessary—to maximize market value. Additionally, apartment buildings tend to have more density than commercial buildings. That means that you have a lot more individual residents on shorter term leases. That gives you more flexibility to adjust to changing markets. Conversely, you can require longer term leases in a market that is having a downturn in order to minimize your losses.

Net operating income for an investment property is determined by subtracting your expenses from your income, and it's the primary indicator for the value of a property.

Income – Expenses = Net Operating Income
Net Operating Income – Mortgage = CASH FLOW

Finding out the value of a property is simply a matter of dividing its net operating income, NOI, by the going capitalization rate. A capitalization rate—commonly referred to as a "cap rate"—is the NOI divided by the purchase price or value of a property. Capitalization rates are determined by evaluating recent sales statistics of similar properties in a given market. Your broker will be a valuable tool in determining your market's capitalization rate.

If you have a property with an annual $100,000 NOI in a market where the capitalization rate is 6 percent, then the value of that property would be $1.66 million. Your equation would look like this:

NOI ($100,000) ÷ Capitalization Rate (6%) = Asset Value ($1.66 million)

One of the biggest advantages of multifamily investment is that you can quickly and dramatically increase the value of an acquisition by increasing its net operating income with sound management principles. That means you can quickly realize the benefits of refinancing the property and reinvesting the equity into other multifamily investments. Later in the book, I'll show you some real-world examples of buildings that Robert and Kim Kiyosaki and I have purchased together and how we quickly turned poor-performing properties into incredible investments with huge returns.

#2. Demand

People always need a place to live. Shelter is one of the basic requirements of existence. That alone gives multifamily an advantage over other types of real estate investments. You can rest assured knowing that there will always be a demand for residential housing whether the market is going up or down.

Besides the fact that there has always traditionally been a huge demand for rental housing, there are a number of factors that will cause demand to soar even higher in the next decade.

ECHO BOOMERS

The echo boomer group is comprised of individuals born between 1982 and 1995. It is estimated that there are around 80 million echo boomers, making them the largest demographic group in the United States since the 1960s. As a group they comprise over one-third of the total U.S. population. The media has labeled them echo boomers because they are the offspring, the "echo," of the last great population surge in America, the baby boomers.

> **Over the next decade the largest demographic group in forty years will be flooding the rental market.**

The reason echo boomers are so significant is because over the next decade approximately 4 million of them will become adults each year. According to a study generated by Harvard University's Joint Center for Housing Studies, 80 percent of all households whose residents are under the age of twenty-five are renters, and 65 percent of those with residents ages twenty-five to twenty-nine are renters. That's a lot of renters!

BABY BOOMERS

There is little doubt that you have heard of this cohort. Until their children, the echo boomers, came along, baby boomers were by far the largest demographic in American history, generally estimated to number about 78 million. Though there are conflicting definitions, baby boomers are generally considered to have been born between the 1940s and 1960s. The first individuals born in this era are just now beginning to reach retirement age.

According to the same Harvard study, a large portion of adults aged sixty-five and older are renters. Currently, 4.1 million households aged sixty-five or older rent in the United States. That number will grow exponentially in the coming years as more and more of the 78 million baby boomers begin to retire. According to an article by the National Association of Realtors, 19 percent of all baby boomers are renters and 37 percent say that they have difficulty making ends meet. Many of these households rely on dual incomes. It is inevitable that the financial pressures of retirement will force some of these households to rent after retirement.

Retiring baby boomers will thus be an important factor in the rental market in the coming years. I'm invested in this demographic, and believe one of the best investments is active adult communities.

In my first book, *The ABC's of Real Estate Investing*, I wrote about my building in Sun City, Arizona. I purchased this property specifically because of the coming baby boomer rental market. Today, that property is my single greatest performer and one of the greatest investments I've ever made. The building is full and there is a paid wait list for those who want to live there. In the next chapter, I'll go into detail about how we acquired the building and our business plan that made it such a success. I've only owned the building for five years, and already I have been able to refinance it and offer huge returns to my investors and myself. Returns that have allowed me to expand my existing portfolio by over 1,000 units! You better believe that I'll be buying more properties just like it.

Together, the echo and baby boomer generations number 158 million households and comprise two-thirds of the entire U.S. population. It is projected that 65 percent of the echo boomers will be renters (52 million) and that at least the current percentage of 19 percent of baby boomers will continue to rent (14.8 million)—that equates to just under 67 million renters. That is in addition to the 34.1 million households that currently rent (it's a safe bet that these cohorts won't be looking to rent commercial space anytime soon). This will apply huge upward pressure on occupancy and rental rates. We may be seeing the beginning of the golden age of multifamily housing. Numbers like those make it seem like Christmas every day to landlords such as myself. And as if that weren't enough, there is one more demographic group that will have a huge demand for rental housing: immigrants.

IMMIGRANTS

Once again we'll turn to our trusty Harvard study to shed some light on why the immigrant population is so significant to the rental market. According to the study, immigrant populations were responsible for 45 percent of all rental growth between 1994 and 2004. It's no lie—immigrants have become a major force in the multifamily market.

Since the 1960s, the number of immigrants entering the United States has grown each decade. In the 1990s alone, 10 million immigrants entered the United States—and those are just the legal ones. Hispanics account for nearly half of all immigration, making me feel pretty good about being based in the Southwest. As of 2006, the United States accepts more immigrants into its borders than the entire world combined. Between 1990 and 2000 the immigrant population in the United States rose by 57.4 percent according to the U.S. Census. And immigration is expected to continue growing in the next decade. Below is a chart of expected immigration through 2010.

Projected Immigrant Growth in the United States				
	Per Year	**2000**	**2004**	**2010**
Immigrant Growth	940,000	31,100,000	34,860,000	40,500,000
Historical Data from 2000 U.S. Census and 2004 Yearbook of Immigrant Statistics				

Are you ready for the final tally? According to the U.S. Census, only 34.9 percent of noncitizen residents are homeowners. That means 65 percent of the immigrant households rent. Based on the immigration chart above, by 2010 an estimated 26.3 million immigrants will be renters. Add that to our earlier numbers of 52 million echo boomers, and 14.8 million baby boomers. Doing so shows you that an estimated 93 million renters will be added to the market over the coming years. Numbers like that simply can't be beat in any other sector of the real estate market.

3. Affordability

Rental housing is cheap—cheap to rent and cheap to buy. I've already established the primacy of leverage when it comes to real estate investments. The good news is leverage makes investing in real estate, especially multifamily, extremely affordable. In any given purchase you only have to come up with around 20 percent of the total asset value in order to experience the benefits of a multifamily investment. Take my recent acquisition in Flagstaff, Arizona, for example. That was a $19.7 million acquisition. I only had to invest a bit over $4 million to secure it—most of which was from investors, a concept we'll explore later in the book.

Real estate is one of the only investments you can buy that is often immediately worth many times more than what you have invested. If I had invested my $4 million into a mutual fund or a stock I would have had . . . $4 million worth of stock. By placing my money in a multifamily investment I immediately had an investment worth $19.7 million—80 percent more than my initial investment. As I discussed earlier, the appreciation I receive from my $19.7 million investment is not based on my actual cash, or my $4 million investment, but on the value of the total asset. At the appreciation rate of 6 percent, that means the total appreciation for just one year on my total asset value of $19.7 million works out to be $1,182,000 versus the same total appreciation on my down payment of $4 million, which is $240,000. That's a difference of $942,000! The bank doesn't get a cent of that. I'm effectively using the bank's money to compound my returns five times over my actual investment. I can't think of cheaper money than that, can you?

4. Business Cycles

Multifamily investments are one of the only sectors of real estate investment that aren't affected by business cycles traditionally viewed as negative like rising interest rates—*if* you already own the property. In fact, rising interest rates are a godsend to a landlord.

As interest rates rise, homes becomes less affordable. What does that do? It makes demand for rental housing even higher because it becomes the affordable option. As demand increases, occupancy and rents increase. This is not the case for single-family housing or commercial real estate. For commercial real estate investors, when housing becomes more expensive, market conditions become more strained. This is because given the choice between allocating income to housing—a basic human need—and an office, a potential resident will choose housing. They might even set up a home office.

5. Maintenance

In addition to the market advantages there are also some operational advantages to investing in multifamily buildings. The maintenance is much less sophisticated than in commercial buildings. In an average multifamily property most maintenance issues can be fixed by an on-site technician. The salaries for these technicians are generally fairly low and any issues that can't be addressed by the on-site maintenance staff can be handled by a relatively inexpensive vendor.

In other types of real estate investments the amount of maintenance work that needs to be done is generally less frequent but much larger in scale. In a commercial building you may not have to do any maintenance projects for months. That makes it extremely unaffordable for an owner to have maintenance staff on-site. That's important because when you finally do have to fix or replace an item, you have to hire outside services. Outside services are expensive.

On larger multifamily properties, however, the amount of maintenance work that is required to keep operations running smoothly will generally support the need for an on-site technician. When something needs to be fixed, you can have your technician take care of it the same day—and at a very low hourly wage. There is no middleman.

In multifamily, the "turning" of a unit takes much less time and is much more affordable than in other real estate investments. Turning a unit refers to the process of cleaning and repairing the unit when a resident moves out so that it can be rented again. On a professionally managed property, a unit can usually be turned in less than three days. The cost is generally minimal.

Additionally, in multifamily properties, residents have no say in how the unit is structured, or how it looks, when they move in. The product is the product. And if it's clean, well kept, well maintained, and there's no damage to the interior, the resident is happy—or should be. Compare this to commercial real estate where owners have to deal with resident improvements. In commercial real estate, every aspect of the lease is negotiated. This includes the interior of the leased space. Each business will have special needs and desires on how they wish to manipulate the space and it's generally very costly. The structuring of this space is called tenant improvements. The cost is almost always borne by both parties—the owner and the tenant.

I have a friend who owns a very successful restaurant in the Phoenix area. She's being pursued by a high-end commercial developer in the city to move her restaurant to their commercial center. The cost to her would be great. She estimates that in order to get the new space improved to her standards it would be over $1.5 million. Both parties have been negotiating on how to handle the cost of this move. Because she has a loyal following in the city, the developer is motivated to have her restaurant become part of their retail center. Consequently, they are negotiating the amount of credit they will give her toward resident improvements. When all is said and done they will be giving her $1 million more just to move into the space. In apartments I sometimes give people a gift basket to move in. But only if I have to.

Personal Plan to Wealth

There are a variety of properties that fall under the category of multifamily. Primarily this book focuses on medium to large apartment building acquisitions ranging from fifty units or more. But that doesn't mean investments in smaller multifamily properties aren't a good move. Even if you purchase a duplex, it's still a better investment than most other options out there. My example earlier in the book of a $200,000 acquisition is evidence of that. The principles of cash flow, leverage, and adding value through sound property management are relevant to any property no matter the size. And the demographics I've laid out in this chapter are equally relevant.

A distinct advantage of multifamily investing is that you can tap into any of the property sizes out there to start building your wealth. You could acquire a four-plex or a 300-unit building. There aren't many commercial real estate investment properties that can be purchased for under $1 million. But there are plenty in the multifamily sector. Just think about it. How many commercial properties—even small ones—are there for under $1 million? Not many that I can think of. That makes multifamily readily accessible to just about anyone looking to invest.

If you have a desire to purchase a large multifamily building, all it requires is a great investment team and a little patience and planning on your part. It's a smart play to invest in any size multifamily property because the returns from that investment will enable you to roll into larger investments down the road.

I have business acquaintances that have expressed a desire to invest in large multifamily acquisitions. Many of them own multiple single-family houses or small multi-unit buildings like duplexes or four-plexes. Thanks to the IRS there are two ways that they (and you) can take existing investments and roll them into larger investments tax-free. You can either:

1. Pull out equity through a refinance, or
2. You can sell your properties and do a 1031 exchange.

Refinancing

Refinancing is a valid option if you have the ability to cover the new mortgage that your smaller properties will have from obtaining new loans. Chances are, however, that your smaller properties will not be able to cash-flow once the equity is drawn.

Look at it this way. If you have ten properties like the $200,000 property we used as an example earlier in the book, you would have a total portfolio valued at $2 million. That is a pretty awesome portfolio. Each one of those properties, however, carries its own mortgage. That means that if you were to refinance all ten properties five years after you purchased them, all ten loans would be higher. Since appreciation on average is higher than rent growth, you would probably not be able to cash-flow on the properties anymore.

For this example we'll assume you had an interest-only loan on the ten properties with an interest rate of 6.5 percent. That means that for each property, you carried a mortgage payment of $867 per month. If you recall the example from Chapter 1, when looking at appreciation, we assumed 4 percent rent growth. That means that the initial $1,000 per month rent is now $1,170 per month after five years. Here is a simple operating statement to show how they would cash-flow based on those numbers:

Rental Income	$ 1,170
Operating Expenses (Insurance, Maintenance, etc.)	$ 250
Mortgage Payment	$ 867
Cash Flow	$ 53

Great news! You are realizing $53 per month in cash flow for each property *before* the refinance. That is $6,360 per year for all ten units. You are on your way toward becoming financially free.

Using our thirty-year appreciation table from earlier in the book, let's assume that we refinance the properties after five years, assuming 6 percent appreciation per year. At that point you would have $52,495 in equity in each unit. That equates to total equity of $524,950 on all ten properties, 80 percent of which you can pull out of your investment as cash on a refinance. Now that's a large chunk of cash to invest. That's a good thing. But let me show you why you wouldn't be able to count on cash flow from those ten properties any longer.

Let's examine what happens to these numbers after a refinance. We'll assume the same interest rate—though it could be higher or lower, there is no way to determine this. The bank will give you up to 80 percent of your equity in a new loan. Since you want to pull out all the equity for investing you can, you will be obtaining loans in the amount of $252,495 on each property, and pulling out 80 percent of the $52,495 of equity in each unit—that is $41,996 per unit and $419,960 total. The new loan changes the monthly mortgage payment to $1,094 for each unit. Here is how the financial statement looks now:

Rental Income	$ 1,170
*Operating Expenses (Insurance, Maintenance, etc.)	$ 300
Mortgage Payment	$ 1,094
Cash Flow	$ (224)

*Expenses adjusted for inflation

Ouch! While you are in a position to substantially expand you investment portfolio, you are also paying $224 per month out of pocket to operate each of your ten properties—that's $26,880 a year! You are not going to be financially free with cash flow like that.

1031 Exchange

On the flip side, by utilizing a 1031 exchange you can roll your properties into one or two larger properties that can sustain the larger debt. Earlier we explored the concept of a 1031 exchange as a like-for-like tax-deferred movement of the gains from one property into another.

As Gary Gorman's example showed us, the 1031 allows you to gradually purchase larger and more expensive deals over a period of time by rolling your appreciation into another property. The beauty of this is that it is tax-deferred and you don't have to leverage the new property as heavily as you would with a refinance. This will allow you to purchase bigger and better properties that will still cash-flow.

Chapter 3

The Real World

So far we've looked at the wealthy and how they attained their wealth, compared real estate investments to other types of investments, and established multifamily as the crème de la crème of real estate investments. By now you should be getting pretty excited about the prospect of investing in multifamily properties.

Up until now, however, we've been going over some concepts that were more cerebral in nature. There have been a lot of numbers and principles, but not necessarily much application. Well, now it's time to roll up our sleeves and put into practice the knowledge.

Working with Robert Kiyosaki and the *Rich Dad* team has been an absolutely awesome experience. Over the past five years, I have traveled with Robert and the *Rich Dad* team all over the world teaching people just like you how they can become financially free. I've also had the privilege to invest with Robert and Kim on some of my own property acquisitions. In this chapter I'm going to tell you about two properties that the Kiyosakis and I purchased as multifamily investments together.

Each property had its own play. There was a game plan we executed each time, consciously working toward maximizing the property's net operating income potential. Every deal is different, and will require a different business plan in order to make it a success. In each of the properties that follow I will show you how we found the opportunity, what our business plan was for the property, how we executed the plan, and what happened after executing the plan.

Then, with that as the foundation, I will spend the rest of the book teaching you how to acquire a building of your own. We'll cover the search process, how to finance your investment, finding a team and investors, due diligence, legal setup, and more. I'll walk you through a large multifamily acquisition all the way to the closing table. By the end of the book, you will feel equipped and confident to find, acquire, and operate your own multifamily investment.

Edgewood—The Construction Play

THE OPPORTUNITY

Edgewood is a property that my company purchased in Tucson, Arizona, with Robert and Kim Kiyosaki as investment partners. We purchased the building in 1999 as a nonlisted transaction. That means that we didn't have to pay any brokerage commissions because technically the property wasn't for sale.

At the time, my company was managing the building for a fee from the owner. Consequently we knew the operations of the property very well and were able to determine a fair market value for the property because we had access to the financials. The building was 144 units. The property, however, had an adjoining ten-acre piece of land that was zoned for multifamily housing. We saw a golden opportunity.

THE PLAN

Our plan was very simple. We would purchase the property at an amount that would be determined by the property's current net operating income along with the adjoining piece of land. We would then develop the land and build a new set of units to increase the size of the apartment community. We own a construction company so we knew we would be able to do this at our cost. Additionally, we knew that we could obtain the existing property at a reasonable price since it was unlisted and we didn't have to compete with other buyers. We were able to review all the financial information and make an offer to the owner. In real estate some of the best deals I've ever made involved properties that never saw the light of day at a brokerage. Don't be afraid to pursue a property just because it isn't listed. Everything is for sale. It just has to be the right price. Here's how we executed the plan.

Step One: We negotiated a deal with the current seller of $7.1 million for the existing apartment community and $500,000 for the adjoining land. All together, the total purchase price of the acquisition was $7.6 million—just a little over $50,000 per unit.

A question I hear a lot when I speak to people at *Rich Dad* seminars on making offers for unlisted buildings is, "How do you know what the price is if it isn't listed?" In my first book I go into great depth on the subject, so I won't burden you now with a bunch of details. But, in short, determining the value of a property is never based on its listing price. The real value of the property is always based on its operating performance. The golden ticket is the net operating income—the NOI. The value of a property is determined by dividing the property's net operating income by the market's capitalization rate. There is no need for you to try to figure out what a market's capitalization rate is. You can get that from your local broker. They will have all the market information needed to supply you with it. All you need to know and remember is that the value of a property is based on its NOI divided by the capitalization rate.

Since we were the management company for the property we had access to the financials and a good relationship with the owner. We were able to use the actual financials from the property and divide the net operating income from the financials by the market capitalization rate. That is how we determined our offer price. It was really as simple as that.

After my team and I had determined what our offering price was going to be, we drafted a letter of intent (LOI) to the owner detailing the terms of our offer. The purpose of the LOI is to negotiate the basic terms of the deal before moving to a purchase and sale agreement, the PSA. You can find sample LOIs on my Web site, kenmcelroy.com. The owner was pleasantly surprised to receive our offer. He wasn't really thinking of selling the property, and now he had an opportunity to realize millions over what he owed on the property. Not everyone will be as accommodating. But you shouldn't let that deter you from making offers on properties that you think will be a great investment.

Once the letter of intent was accepted we moved into the purchase and sale agreement negotiations. Since the LOI only has the basic terms for the purchase and sale agreement, we then had to flush out the details. Never, and I mean never, try to negotiate a purchase and sale agreement on a large deal without the help of good, qualified legal counsel. The negotiation of the purchase and sale agreement is critical because it's the document that will spell out the purchase price, time frame of the deal, the amount of money required as deposits and stipulate when those deposits will become nonrefundable.

Step Two: Once we had reached acceptable terms on the purchase and sale agreement, my partners and I executed the agreement and placed the property in escrow. In order to do this we put a refundable deposit up that was contingent on our due diligence period and financing. Due diligence is something that I'll explain in more depth later in the book. Briefly, it is the period of time that you have to explore every aspect of the property. You should dig deep during this period. It should be a good amount of time so that you can be thorough. I like to have at least a month to perform my due diligence. It's important because your findings in the due diligence period will determine whether you are getting what was promised, can ask for a price reduction, or even whether you should walk away from a deal. The best part is that—provided you structured your purchase and sale agreement correctly—in case you find something you don't like, you can take your deposit and walk. No harm, no foul.

During our due diligence period we focused both on the property itself and the adjacent land. As I've said, residential property was fairly easy for us to analyze since we had been managing it for years. We knew pretty much everything there was to know. The adjacent property was another matter. We knew that we wanted to develop the land so that we could build another set of apartments to complement the existing ones, but we didn't know the extent to which we would be able to do that. Over the due diligence period we had a series of meetings with architects, engineers, subcontractors, and city planners to determine what exactly could be done on our potential parcel of land. When we were finished, we knew we could get approval to build 108 extra units and make the overall property a 252-unit apartment community. To obtain financing for the entire project, we contacted several mortgage brokers and began to gather quotes for our loan.

Step Three: After meeting with and receiving bids from the architects, engineers, subcontractors, and the city, we were able to put together a rough construction budget and estimated cost of building the new 108 units.

Once we had a construction budget based on our bids, we developed a timeline for the construction. Having both a timeline and a budget are important because you can't get a construction loan without them. You need to be able to show a potential lender what your plan is and that you have thought it out completely. A plan by itself is not enough. The timeline determines the way in which the lender will distribute the money to you. When you are building a large project like an apartment building, the lender doesn't just release all the money to you. That would be foolish, since there would be no asset for them to take if you were to run out of money before the project was finished. Instead, a lender releases money through "draws," where the loan funds are released from the lender based upon specific, predetermined criteria such as paid invoices and lien releases from contractors and vendors. That way we could be assured as well as the lender that we would have funds available when we needed them.

Step Four: We were beginning to get excited about this project and the potential to provide our investors substantial gains because we would build the property at cost. We had already determined our purchase price, made our offer through a letter of intent, negotiated a purchase and sale agreement, performed due diligence, and started a construction plan. Now we needed to take our vision and find a lender that was the right fit.

In the meantime our due diligence team verified the leases, service contracts, and walked all the units to look for any potential issues. The management team completed a first-year operating budget both for the 144 units and our soon to be new 108 units. Because the new property would be 100 percent vacant when complete, a "lease up" budget was created to estimate the cash flow needs while we filled it with new residents.

We went about determining the amount of leverage that the property could reasonably sustain. When you are using OPM (Other People's Money) for a multifamily investment you want to be sure that the operations of the property can pay for the mortgage and still provide a good return to the investors. Depending on the property, that might be a 70 percent loan or an

80 percent loan. There is no absolutely right ratio. It will depend on your financial analysis and what you feel the operations will be able to sustain. Ultimately you need to know that the decision for what kind of leverage the property can sustain will be determined by the lender's underwriting department, not you. But having a number in mind will help you more effectively shop for the right loan through your mortgage broker and obtain multiple quotes with differing interest rates, loan terms, and leverage percentages.

Once we were able to decide what kind of leverage we wanted to have for the property we began to review our quotes. The goal when shopping for a loan is to find one that works best for both you and your investors. Don't just settle for the first term sheet you get from a lender. Use those term sheets to play one lender off another. Make them compete for your business. By looking at a variety of loan options, you will have a much better chance of starting off on the right foot when you take possession of the property at close of escrow. We reviewed the operating budget and the construction budget with our potential lenders. They are often valuable resources for analyzing your deal because they technically have a 70 to 80 percent stake in the property and therefore have a vested interest in the success of your business plan. Don't be surprised if a lender requests changes to the business plan to suit his or her investment needs.

At this point we also contacted our lawyer so that he could begin the process of forming the legal entity that the property would operate under. I always place any investment property that I acquire into a single-purpose entity, like a limited liability company (LLC). Doing so helps to further ensure that my company will be protected from any litigation. As I mentioned earlier, never have all your eggs in one basket; you should have all your properties under individual entities.

Step Five: Once we found the loan we were looking for, we had all the information we needed to present our investment opportunity to our investors. We had a property in escrow under a purchase and sale agreement, the start of a business plan that included a detailed construction plan for the adjoining land, and the financing terms. The only remaining task was to actually raise the remaining equity for the down payment. We do this on all our deals through an investment summary. An investment summary is a business plan that outlines all the pertinent details of a deal in an easy-to-read document for review by our accredited investors. An accredited investor is someone who is in a financial position to invest a substantial sum of money in a project. To be accredited, he or she doesn't have to be super-rich, but he or she must have a net worth of $1 million or more or make over $200,000 a year ($300,000 if married). Essentially, an accredited investor should be able to absorb any losses that might occur. Later in the book, I'll go into more detail on this concept.

Typically an investment summary should include the following:

- Information about the nature of the investment. There is risk involved and you should disclose this fact up front. Also be sure to mention the fact that any information released by you to an investor is for them only to evaluate and that it's confidential.
- Language detailing the qualifications required to be considered an accredited investor—i.e., someone who has enough money as detailed above to invest in the project without putting themselves at risk of bankruptcy. If you take on unaccredited investors, meaning those who fall below the accredited thresholds, you need additional legal documents.
- A description of the limited liability company. Disclose the name of the LLC and what the purpose of the entity is. This should be a single-asset entity. The purpose is to operate the investment and to provide the investor with both their equity and a return on that equity.
- A quick description of the property, detailing the type of property it is (garden-style apartment, mid-rise, high-rise, four-plex, etc.). Should also include a description of when it was built, how many units there are and a breakdown of the units, the area the property is in, and any types of amenities or qualities the property has.
- Disclosure of the process of the acquisition and the final negotiated purchase price of the property.
- Detailed description that includes the process you used for the due diligence and the reasoning behind it. Describe what you found in the due diligence period, the ramifications and cost, and the plan for addressing those findings. Also, include your financial analysis for review and give a description of how you plan to achieve your projected numbers.

- All the information possible on the financing. The terms, amount, all uses of the money and the sources of the money.
- A picture of the estimated cash flow and the way in which profits will be distributed.
- An index with pictures of the property, market information, and any articles on the economic activity in the market that might help you in your process of raising equity.

Remember that you are selling the investment to the investor. They don't have any obligation to give you their money. You have to give them reasons. If you have a good deal, this should be easy. For an example of an investor summary, you can visit my Web site (kenmcelroy.com) and download one from my previous deals.

Step Six: Our business plan and our discussions with lenders helped us determine the amount of equity we would need to acquire the property. In the case of this property, we needed a little over $2.7 million to cover our down payment and initial start-up construction costs. We didn't have a lot of time to raise the money but we knew that it would be easy because of its significant upside. What it did require, however, was detail-oriented coordination. We had to form a database with the contact information of all the people that were interested in investing in the property and contact each one to determine their level of interest in the acquisition. On the spreadsheet we tracked the potential equity contributions that they indicated to us. This gave us an idea of how much equity we had raised at any given moment.

This is a delicate balancing act. You want to raise just the right amount of money needed to finance the deal. Later in the book I'll run through the details of this process. In the case of this property—and with most of our investment offerings—we had to turn people away who wanted to invest with us because we had all the money we needed. Once our investors committed the needed equity amount, we sent them legal documents for submitting their equity commitments and sending their money to use. We placed all funds in a trust account for the day of closing.

As the documents and, more importantly, the money, began to roll in, we noted that on our spreadsheet as well. It was a valuable tool because we were always able to see on one page the status of the entire deal as it pertained to our equity. As the days drew nearer and nearer to closing we were constantly communicating with our investors, letting them know the timetable of the transaction and reminding those that hadn't gotten their money in to do so.

Step Seven: We closed escrow. This is where the hard work of the past months came to fruition. We had the money we needed and all that remained was for my partner, Ross, and I to sign the documents.

EXECUTION

Now that we owned the property, we had to execute our business plan to successfully bring returns to ourselves and our investors. That is always an exhilarating and scary time. But as with all our acquisitions, we hit the ground running the day we signed the closing documents. From that point on there were a number of balls in the air that we needed to manage, and manage effectively. We now owned 144 units. We had to manage these units to the budget that we promised to our investors. Not only that, we were building the 108 units on the adjoining lot. There was a tight deadline. Our goal was to begin construction immediately and obtain the certificate of occupancy for the first finished building within nine to ten months. That meant we had to be Johnny-on-the-spot when it came to interacting with the city and each of the companies we were using for various aspects of the construction.

In order to begin construction, the city required us to pull permits. That meant filling out all sorts of mind-numbing paperwork and applications—and waiting. And waiting some more. Once we had final approval, we coordinated with our subcontractors and managed the process of construction from the ground up. As we finished buildings and obtained the certificates of occupancy, we turned over the buildings to our property management team based on a predetermined construction schedule. They in turn walked all the buildings, examining the interiors and the exteriors. From their walks they determined any unfinished construction items—commonly referred to as "punch" items—that needed to be completed before they took full possession of the building.

In the meantime, our management company was still operating the original 144 units. They were taking care of the leasing and maintenance, and managing the property to budget so that we could make sure to increase the value of the existing asset for our investors. They were also beginning to rent the new 108 units. This required a separate budget and marketing plan. Believe me, the property manager had her hands full, coordinating the construction company, residents, and potential residents, since the goal was to keep leasing the original property, but also to be preleasing the new units. Once a building was turned over to the property management, we wanted as many preleases as possible so that residents could move in right away and we could minimize lost potential income. Eventually all the buildings were delivered to the property management team and they had the task of managing the existing property and filling up the new one. It was quite the juggling act, but one they did well.

REFINANCE—GIVING BACK THE LOVE

The goal all along was to continue the successful operations of the 144 units and create value through the addition of the 108 newly constructed units. We also had the added benefit of purchasing the building in Tucson, where the market was just beginning to take off. Once we had finished the construction of the new units and had been operating the property for a couple of years, we knew it was time to refinance the property and take advantage of the tax benefits by pulling out and distributing some of the value to our investors.

In a refinance the first thing you do is contact lenders and obtain quotes. At the same time you will be analyzing the property's operations to determine what kind of new loan the property can sustain. The higher mortgage payment should not be a problem because, as a result of sound management, the cash flow is higher on the property than when you purchased it. Once you have obtained quotes, review the interest rates, the closing costs, and analyze how the new loan will affect cash flow. Then all you have to do is pick the best loan quote for your needs and move forward with the lender.

In the case of Edgewood, the value of the property had risen through sound property management and the addition of the 108 units. Additionally, rents had risen in the Tucson market by 7 percent in the three short years since we had purchased the property. Talk about good timing. Because of these factors we were able to refinance the property for $10.5 million—nearly $3 million more than we had purchased the property for. With that refinance we were able to pay off the existing loan for the property and the construction loan we had obtained to build the 108 units, and combine them into one loan. We actually had a lower mortgage payment when we did this since we were not paying interest on a construction loan, which is typically higher than a multifamily loan. Additionally, we had left close to $500,000—all of which was tax-free—that we were able to distribute to our investors. Now repositioned with a lower debt payment and outstanding operating performance, we were already looking ahead to our next goal: to refinance the property again a couple years later (again tax-free) and return both the rest of the original equity invested *and* a return on that equity.

We just recently finished refinancing Edgewood for the second time, and boy was it worth the wait. Remember our plan? We purchased the 144 units, built 108 more, operated the property successfully, refinanced to pay for the additional 108 units tax-free, and now we were refinancing for pure profit—m y favorite thing. When all was said and done, we were able to refinance the property the second time around for $15.6 million. That is a full $8 million higher than the original purchase price, and $5 million over the last refinance. With this tax-free money, we were able to return all the original equity for the deal to our investors, plus a substantial profit on that money. All in all, our investors made 40 percent on their money, not including depreciation and tax savings, which depended on their own situations and the amounts they invested. The investors now have absolutely NO money invested in the property and they continue to receive a percentage of the cash flow. It is free money that simply lands in their accounts each month.

Fountains at Sun City—The Operations Play

THE OPPORTUNITY
We purchased Fountains at Sun City in 2000 for $9 million. The seller was a New York City billionaire that had developed the property and was selling it fairly new. The property is a 182-unit retirement community that only accepts residents who are 55 and over. It's in one of the hottest active adult communities in the Phoenix metropolitan area, Sun City, which is the largest and first of its kind in the country.

At the time when we purchased the property, though, it wasn't highly occupied because of the age restriction. Thus, despite it being a new, attractive development, leasing was slow and occupancy was low. We were interested in active adult housing, however, because we knew that the first wave of baby boomers were just getting ready to retire. We felt that we would be able to raise the occupancy rate as more and more baby boomers retired and moved to Arizona's warmer climate. Besides upping our rental income, we knew that increased occupancy would also make the property more valuable.

THE PLAN

Step One: From our due diligence, we knew that the rents were lower than the rest of the market and the occupancy was low. We determined this from a market survey that took less than a day. Our plan was a very simple one— increase rents to market and increase occupancy. Additionally, we planned to add more services for the residents in order to attract more leases and retain the existing residents.

During our due diligence we discovered something exciting. When looking at the vacant units, we noticed that most of them were upstairs. This made sense because most seniors would rather not have to walk up a flight of stairs if it can be avoided. A quick glance at the rent roll showed us that rents were exactly the same whether you rented a unit on the first or second floor. Given the choice, the residents always chose the first floor over the second. We decided to increase the downstairs rents by $50. We also began increasing the rents on renewals.

Very quickly we began to see the second-floor units fill up with seniors who felt saving an extra $50 per month was well worth a trip up the stairs. For us it was a no-brainer. Eventually that $50 increase was applied to all the downstairs units—half the units on the property. That equated to a $4,550 increase in income every month— $54,600 per year. We've already been through this exercise before, but it's so much fun to see how a little change can add up big. By dividing the $54,600 in extra rental income by a 6 percent capitalization rate, we can see that just by raising the bottom-floor rents by $50 we increased the value of the Fountains at Sun City by $910,000 in about a year.

> **$50 a month extra per unit can mean millions in added value. Simple is as simple does.**

Additionally, we discovered the need for better amenities at the property in order to compete effectively in the market. With this in mind, we purchased a 26-passenger van to shuttle the residents around town for shopping, medical needs, and so forth, and hired a full-time activity director. The existing residents were extremely pleased with these additions. And so were we. We saw units rented faster and existing residents didn't want to leave. Occupancy began to grow. Today there is a waiting list to live on the property, some even waiting for months. It's a good problem to have.

Step Two: We were initially worried about the increased expenses that would be incurred by our added amenities. After all, we had to hire a driver for the bus and an activity director. This turned out to be an unnecessary concern. When you have a property full of highly motivated and educated seniors with spare time on their hands, it isn't that hard to find well-educated and motivated employees at a reasonable cost.

For instance, we were able to hire our activity director just by giving a discount on the rent. It worked out perfectly since the person already lived there and knew many of the residents and it was something that she had already wanted to do. The discounted rent was really just an added benefit to being able to organize fun events and interact with her neighbors. In this way, the gains we made from our additions far outweighed the expenses. It was a win-win. The residents were happier and so were we.

We also discovered during our due diligence that expenses were running high on the property because of a bulk agreement for the alarm and cable companies. The current ownership was paying a flat fee per unit every month for these services. That meant that regardless of whether a unit was occupied or not, the owners were still paying for the cable and alarm system. Once we closed on the property, we renegotiated the alarm and cable contract for a savings of over $2,000 per month—$24,000 per year—another $400,000 in value added! There is a lesson to be learned here. Always make sure to evaluate existing service contracts when you purchase a property— you never know what you might find. This was another twofold gain, as the residents were happy with the change in service because the plan now allowed them to order the channels they wanted, whereas they hadn't been able to before.

Step Three: When purchasing the property we looked for a loan that would maximize our leverage. Although the property was relatively new, we knew right off the bat that there were going to be some small capital items that would need to be completed on the property after we closed escrow. This included a paint job and some roof work, which we estimated to be about $200,000, according to the bids we obtained from vendors. We found an excellent loan for $7.2 million, which was 80 percent leverage (the purchase price was $9 million). In raising our equity, we took into account the money that was needed for a down payment ($1.8 million) and the money that was needed for the capital improvements ($200,000). We raised $2 million in equity and purchased the property with very little money out of our own pockets. In return, the investors would get the lion's share of the profits.

EXECUTION

First Year of Operation: By executing on our plan as detailed earlier we were able to increase the income on the property by a whopping $100,000 in the first year of operations at Fountains at Sun City. Based on a 6 percent capitalization rate, that is $1.7 million in added value. This was an amazing feat, considering that in most properties the first year is a transition year, in which very little cash flow is realized.

We did have to lower our net operating income by $40,000 to hire a bus driver and the full-time activity director, but remember that our renegotiation of the existing cable and alarm contracts saved us $24,000. And our increased rents and higher occupancy raised our net operating income by $84,000. That meant that in just the first year of operations we turned a $9 million property into a $10.4 million property. All because of sound property management.

Year Two: In the second year of operations we began to realize the gains from the operational changes that we instituted in year one. The occupancy was now at 92 percent, up from 85 percent when we purchased the property, and by year two we had implemented additional rental increases that we planned in year one. The higher occupancy and increased rents accounted for another $100,000 in gross income.

Of course, just as in year one, however, our expenses increased with our income. These included increases in salaries for the staff, utilities, taxes, and insurance. With the expenses factored in, the net increase in income was about $70,000 for year two. Again, that meant that by using simple, sound property management principles, we had increased the net operating income of the property over two years by $154,000 since we had acquired it. That equated to about $2.6 million in added value.

Year Three: Now that the property was experiencing the benefits of high occupancy and market rents, we decided to kick it up a notch. We instituted a resident utility billing system, commonly referred to as RUBS. The concept behind RUBS is actually fairly new in the apartment industry. It's charging back a portion of the utilities used by the residents.

Under most properties the bulk utilities bills are paid by the landlord. In a property with a RUBS program, however, the electric, water, sewer, gas, and trash expenses are totaled up and sent to the residents on a per unit basis. After all, they are the ones that use the utilities. In essence, the resident reimburses the owner at rent time. The owner still pays the utility bills but realizes income through RUBS to offset the expense. The average monthly usage for each unit was around $45. We started passing these costs onto the residents and since there were 182 units that was over $8,190 in monthly income. Within twelve months (this takes time), this helped increase our income by $98,280 for the year. At the same time rents were continually increased to take advantage of the rent growth in Phoenix of 3 percent per year on average, and occupancy remained high.

By the end of year three and into year four, the property began to significantly cash-flow. The annual cash flow was in excess of $250,000 per year and we were realizing 12.5 percent cash-on-cash rate of return for our investors ($250,000 cash flow ÷ $2,000,000 in equity = 12.5 percent). Not only that, the cash flow was tax-free because of depreciation. We knew it was time to refinance.

REFINANCE

This section will be short and sweet. The appraisal for this community came in at $15 million—$6 million higher than we paid. This time around, we decided to take less of a loan so we could continue to realize excellent cash flow even after the refinance. Our loan, of approximately $12,260,000, was only

70 percent of the appraisal, but over $5 million more than the current loan and over 100 percent more than our initial equity raise of $2 million. We distributed all the proceeds to our investors, which included their initial equity and their return, and pocketed a cool million for ourselves as the developers.

All of this was accomplished through a sound business plan. I love multifamily real estate. I don't have to worry about the value of the properties around me. All I have to worry about is operating my property to its optimal performance. The value of my asset is based on that and that alone. There was no magic trick behind raising the value of Fountains at Sun City by over $6 million. It was a simple roll-up-your-sleeves-and-manage-well endeavor. That is what I call *creating* wealth.

THE FLYWHEEL CONCEPT

In his excellent book *Good to Great,* Jim Collins writes of the Flywheel Concept. A flywheel is a big, heavy metal disc that is mounted horizontally on an axle. In order to get it moving you have to exert a tremendous amount of energy and effort. At first the going is very slow, and very arduous. But then, as you begin to move the wheel, its weight creates momentum. Slowly, with the same amount of effort on your part, the wheel will pick up speed. Eventually, the flywheel will spin at incredible velocity through its own momentum. The work you did earlier is compounded by the weight of the wheel and soon it has a momentum all its own.

Now that our flywheel is in motion, my business partners and I find it easier to seek out deals, finance them, and raise the equity needed to purchase them. We are now a proven entity, and while there is never a guarantee that we will be successful at every turn, our investors trust us with their money. The beauty is that when we refinance or sell a property and return equity to our investors, they don't want it. What I mean is they want to reinvest instead, and they often choose to roll it into another one of our acquisitions. This creates more wealth for them and more wealth for us.

As you become more and more adept at investing in multifamily properties, you, too, will begin to set your own flywheel in motion. It will be a lot of work at first, and sometimes you might feel like giving up, but don't. As the wheel turns, the process will become easier, and your wealth will grow.

Chapter 4

Investing in Apartment Buildings

In this chapter I will debunk the common misconceptions people have about investing in apartment buildings. Then, once we've moved past that, I'll show you how to begin looking for your perfect multifamily investment through my three-part research process. I'll also show you some positive trends and factors you should be looking for when beginning your search for a multifamily investment.

Myth #1: You Need a Lot of Money

This is by far the most common excuse that people give me for not investing in multifamily properties. But it just simply isn't true. You don't need a lot of money. What you do need is a good deal. By a good deal, I mean an investment property that has profit potential and that is based on solid financials. Just by reading this book and continuing your financial education with the *Rich Dad* team you are taking great steps to combat the mind-set that money will fix your problems.

Remember the property I recently purchased in Flagstaff? That building was a $19.7 million deal, and I raised almost all the equity with outside investors, or OPM. You're probably thinking how can that be, since you'll remember that the down payment for that building was around $4 million. But I swear it's true. I had very little money in the deal, yet we own the building.

As I've done so many times before, I gave the majority of the ownership to those who put money down to purchase it. The concept is simple: You find a great apartment investment, raise the equity required to purchase it, and give the equity participants on your team the majority ownership—keeping an interest for yourself.

Many people don't like the idea of partnerships. "I'm leaving too much money on the table," they think to themselves. But nothing could be further from the truth. In a partnership investment, you have much more purchasing power than you would by yourself. That means you can purchase a building that is of higher quality and that has more income-producing potential.

Think of it this way: Maybe by yourself you have $20,000 to invest in a piece of real estate. That means that you can purchase a $100,000 building. Well, first off you aren't going to find many $100,000 multifamily investments available. Secondly, which would you rather have, the $100,000 building that cost you $20,000 in your own cash, or like me, the partnered ownership of a $19.7 million building that cost very little? A 20 percent ownership stake equals out to be $3,940,000—money that I generated out of thin air because I had enough vision to find a great deal and to find investors who were looking for a great deal.

When it came to finding investors for my Flagstaff property, I had to do very little selling. The deal was very good. Here's a secret you should know: There's a nearly inexhaustible supply of people who are looking to invest their money in a good deal. All you need to do is find it and the hardest part is done. Granted, your first deal will be the most difficult, since you don't have a proven track record. But this is where your team comes in, and with each successful deal you will have more and more investors beating down your door to place money with you and your investments.

Myth #2: You Have to Start Small

Often people think that they have to start with a small property and work their way up to a bigger one. First off, that is not a bad strategy, and many people become successful investors by doing so. In fact, my first investment property was a two-bedroom condominium that I furnished and rented out to vacationers. I would say, however, that this is not the best way to go about investing in real estate.

I purchased my two-bedroom condominium before I knew better. The property was $119,000. In order to buy the property I had to put $20,000 of my own money into the property. My risk was more because I alone was responsible for the mortgage payment. Conversely, my Flagstaff property is worth many times more than my two-bedroom condominium but has much less risk since the ownership of the property—and the mortgage—is spread over many individual leases. Also, the size of the property allows for it to be professionally managed.

Many people feel that they cannot qualify for a loan when it comes to larger buildings. That would be the case if it were a single-family house or a condominium you were purchasing as an investment. In those cases, the loan is secured by your personal assets. Even my partner and I had a hard time acquiring a few-hundred-thousand-dollar loan for some small condominiums we purchased in Las Vegas. The problem was we had our money in other real estate assets (since liquidity is something we wanted to avoid). Well, because the property was smaller scale, the bank was looking for cash assets only, so it didn't matter to them that we had multiple millions in real estate assets. However, when it came time to get the multimillion-dollar loan required for our 356-unit acquisition in Oklahoma City, we didn't have any trouble. The lesson here is that larger investment properties are secured by the asset itself because their values are based on performance, and everyone is primarily looking to the property to pay them back through its operations.

As I mentioned earlier, sound property management is the primary way to increase the value of a multifamily property. Suffice it to say, the ability to increase a property's value through operations is a huge advantage over smaller investments. With smaller investments, like single-family houses, the appreciation of the property is based solely on the appreciation of the neighborhood around you. If you did your homework, the appreciation will generally be good, but ultimately that's out of your control. The fact remains that you are not in control of creating the value for the property, the market is.

In both cases from the preceding chapter, the value of those investments was increased by our efforts and some market appreciation. For Edgewood, it was through capital improvements and efficient operations. For Fountains at Sun City it was through simple operational changes that dramatically increased our net operating income. The point is that we had a stake in creating value for the property. We did not have to rely on just the market around us.

With large multifamily buildings you are in complete control of how well your property performs operationally, and thus how much it will appreciate. Even better, you can hire a professional property management company to oversee the operations, whereas on a smaller property you will have much more of your personal time invested. With a larger multifamily investment, a professional property management firm operates your investment for you and sends you the check at the end of the month. That frees you up to keep looking for more deals, which will help you to continue growing your wealth.

Myth #3: You Need the Midas Touch

In *The ABC's of Real Estate Investing*, I wrote about the Midas Touch. It seems that some people have it and others don't. Those with the Midas Touch appear to succeed at everything they put their hand to. The Midas Touch is about as realistic as magic; it's all an illusion. In reality, those who appear to have the Midas Touch are those who know the tricks of the trade and thus know how to spot a good deal when they see one. They also know what it will take to purchase a solid deal and operate it successfully and profitably. In other words, they have studied and learned about investing and finance just the way you are now.

It took me a long time to get to the place where I am today. Just like you, I spent a good portion of my working life trying to earn more money so I could spend it on more things. I didn't have the advantage of being taught financial education like you do now. Slowly, through many years of trial and error,

I earned my stripes on the job. I had built a successful business, but I was still working for others. My money was dependent on my clients. Thankfully, I was able to meet successful, self-made entrepreneurs along the way who were willing to take me under their wing and teach me. And before long, I caught the entrepreneurial bug and haven't looked back since.

Many of you are going through the same process I went through. I commend you for picking up this book, as well as other *Rich Dad* books, and educating yourself. If you continue to learn, and to apply your learning by investing in assets, you, too, will look like you have the Midas Touch. Once you have the knowledge, all successful real estate investing requires is common sense. Equipped with knowledge and the insider tips you will be able to use yours when evaluating a deal. There will be no magic, just know-how.

Myth #4: You Have to Know Somebody

The old business adage goes, "It's not about what you know; it's about who you know." And that's true—in business. It's not necessarily true, however, in investing. You don't need to know anyone connected with real estate investing in order to get started. In investing it's all about *what* you know because what you know will determine *who* you know. Once you have found a good deal, you will be able to attract investors. But in order to find a good deal, you need to know how to spot one.

Here is what I mean. I recently purchased a building in Oklahoma City. I had never been to Oklahoma before I invested there. I didn't know a soul in the city. What I did know was that its economy was on the upswing and the apartment market there was affordable to invest in; therefore, there were some good deals with profit potential. I felt sure I had to invest there. From my office I spent a lot of time reading about Oklahoma City and its submarkets. Then I looked at broker listings and evaluated individual properties. Finally, I found an awesome deal.

The first person I contacted in Oklahoma was the broker who had listed the deal. Through him I was able to get the names of local experts, as well as more up-to-date financials for my operational analysis of the property, and some helpful data on the local market. I then did some Internet research on Oklahoma City property managers, city officials, other brokers, and so on.

Before I ever set foot in Oklahoma City to look at the property, and before I had ever met anyone there, I already had a number of meetings lined up to begin the process of assembling my team. My deal created the opportunity to meet my team members, not the other way around. Hey, "If you build it they will come."

Myth #5: You Have to Be a Seasoned Negotiator

This just isn't true. If you have to "hard-sell" a deal, then it probably isn't a good deal. When you walk into a boardroom or an investor's office your confidence and position of strength will be in the deal itself, not in your ability to present or negotiate it. In my book *The ABC's of Real Estate Investing*, I go into great detail on how, once you find a property, you can evaluate it in order to know the actual value of the deal. Remember, the listed purchase price is usually meaningless. Once you have completed your financial homework on a property and have solid financial numbers to show what a great deal it is, you won't have to do any convincing; the numbers will speak for themselves.

Also keep in mind that what you would probably consider a negotiation meeting is, to me, simply a meeting to present the deal. I've already done all the work. I have the numbers figured out, and I confidently know the value of the property and why it is worth what it is. There are times where my deal may not meet someone's needs. That's okay. There are many others for whom the deal will work. I don't have trouble finding investors for my company's acquisitions. Is it because I'm such a phenomenal and charismatic businessperson? Not even close. Investors for whom the deal is right take one look at the bottom line and sign up. There is no real trick to this other than applying knowledge and being diligent in research. No matter what your personality or your background, you have the ability to put together a great deal and attract investors. You can do this.

Now that we've dispelled the myths that keep people from multifamily investing, I'll spend the rest of the book equipping you with the knowledge you need to actually begin looking for that sweet deal. Then finally I'll show you how to lock up a property in a contract and outline the steps that will take you from a potential investment to the closing table.

Buyer Beware

A word of caution: While there are a lot of people out there who will genuinely want to be part of your team, to take you under their wing and teach you, and who will have your best interest in mind, there are also a lot of people in the industry who are looking to take advantage of you. When evaluating a potential investment property there are a few pitfalls you should be looking to avoid. I've seen a lot of investors lose a lot of money on deals because they didn't have a discerning eye. They trusted, but they didn't verify. If, for whatever reason, you don't feel you have a discerning enough eye, then find someone who does, like a property manager. The number one mistake an investor makes is that they take everything the seller, or the listing broker, says at face value.

Listing Brokers and Selling Brokers

What you need to remember about a listing broker is that they work for the seller, and they are motivated to obtain the highest purchase price. The higher they can drive up the price of a property, the higher their commission. This is the way the game is played, and when the shoe is on the other foot, you will learn to love your listing broker.

As long as you have a clear picture of what motivates them, brokers can be a lot of help. For one thing, it is easy to go to a broker's Web site and sign up to be on their mailing list for markets that you are interested in. Usually, they will be able to e-mail you new listings with flyers on the properties. By filling out a confidentiality agreement, you can obtain valuable financial information about a property you're interested in and the market it's located in. Such documents will assist you in verifying claims made by the listing broker and the seller.

Additionally, larger multifamily brokerages, such as CBRE or Hendricks & Partners, produce market studies with detailed information for a variety of markets all over the United States. You can obtain these for free. I'm on many broker mailing lists. I get investment offerings coming to me in the mail every day. Most of them I don't have the time to review in great detail, but every once in a while a diamond will land on my desk. When that happens I begin my initial research to determine if I want to pursue it. The best part is the information comes to me. The only energy and time I spend is to input my address on a Web site and make a few calls.

Property investment summaries come in a fairly standard format. There is generally a picture of the property on the front along with a listing price and the contact information for the broker. On the back are some numbers that are supposed to indicate the property's operational performance. These generally include a unit mix and rent schedule along with an operational income and expense pro forma projecting the property's operation potential in the coming years.

You should always verify a pro forma that is part of a brokerage investment summary. If you purchase a property off of the pro forma on a brokerage investment summary, it's more than likely you will not make any money from your investment. Rather, you will probably lose money. The reason is this:

Numbers in a seller pro forma are typically based on projections, *not* performance.

On the back of many broker sales brochures, the following or similar words are almost always printed on the bottom: "This brokerage company makes no warranty or representation about the content of this brochure. It is your responsibility to independently confirm its accuracy and competencies. Any projections, opinions, assumptions, or estimates used are for example only and do not represent the current or future performance of the property."

I call buying a property at what it *could* operate at buying "retail." Never buy retail. Rather you want to purchase an investment at "wholesale." That means basing your offering price on what the property's current net operating income is. If you decide to trust what the broker is saying in their investment summary you can't blame anyone but yourself if the deal doesn't pan out the way you expected. Later, we'll go into detail about how to obtain accurate information, and I'll give you my personal system for determining the true value of a property. For now I want to tell you a story to show you just how dangerous it can be to trust the information provided by a broker instead of trusting but verifying.

I got a call from an investor a few years back who had a bit of panic in his voice. He was purchasing a multifamily property in Mesa, Arizona, and needed to hire a property management company.

"Great," I told him. "When do you want to schedule a meeting?"

"I close on the property tomorrow," he responded.

"This won't be good," I thought to myself. The investor was from California and had sold one of his other properties. Wanting to defer his tax liability, he was moving the money via a 1031 exchange and had purchased the property in Mesa based on the listing broker's pro forma. Now he was calling us to take over the management of a property the next day! Needless to say, that's not a good idea when you purchase your property. It usually takes a month or more to transition into managing a property effectively.

We did take over management of the property to help out the investor. Quickly it became evident that he had made a poor choice. Just by reviewing the actual property financial statements we knew he had overpaid for the property by $2 million. The property was in bad shape. There was over $200,000 in deferred maintenance issues that we discovered and the resident profile was very bad. Right away we had to begin eviction proceedings on over twenty residents—and the property was only 80 percent occupied as it was.

The investor made a hasty decision and paid for it dearly. If he had taken the time to verify the claims of the seller and the listing broker, he would have discovered many of these issues well before he ever owned the building. Instead he lost millions of dollars.

Sellers with Bad Management

Properties that have been managed poorly are a double-edged sword. On one hand, they can be an incredible deal; on the other, they can be a huge money pit. It ultimately depends on what *type* of bad management we're talking about. I drool over deals where the owner simply didn't know what he was doing. If you look hard enough you'll be able to find properties where the owner doesn't know the market or hasn't been paying attention. With such properties come many untapped opportunities for generating income and lowering expenses.

Once again, I have to turn to my Flagstaff acquisition as an example. Among the many things we discovered when doing our due diligence was that the management company had implemented resident utility bill-backs, or RUBS (resident utility billing system), on the property. As I mentioned earlier, RUBS are a way to dramatically increase your property's income earning potential by collecting a metered fee from the residents for utilities. Well, the management did the right thing by implementing RUBS, but they executed it completely wrong. Instead of instituting RUBS on top of the rents, they reduced the rents to cover the added cost of the utilities. They were afraid that people would move away.

Our market survey, however, revealed that not only was every competing property charging RUBS on top of the monthly market rent, they were also charging more in rent than the rent on our potential property *before* they reduced the rental amount to compensate for the added RUBS. When all was said and done, our potential property's rents ended up being on average $45 per unit below market. The property is 278 units. That means the management company was losing $150,120 per year in income just by not being diligent in keeping up with the market. Based on a capitalization rate of 6 percent, that works out to $2,502,000 in lost value that we were able to reclaim just by raising rents to market level after we acquired the building. In this case we took advantage of another owner's management oversight to create value quickly and easily.

There is another type of bad management, however, that you need to avoid dealing with at all cost. That is *negligent* management. Management that is intentionally negligent will oftentimes do irreparable damage to an asset. The biggest culprit you'll find will be deferred maintenance. Purchasing a property that has deferred maintenance is not always a bad play, but it is always a costly one—both in time and in money.

Deferred maintenance is maintenance that should have been completed but that has been put off, and put off, and put off in order to "save" money. I put save in quotation marks because the only person deferred maintenance saves money is the owner who is lucky enough to find a sucker to purchase his property. I can't stress enough the importance of doing a thorough and proper due diligence before you buy a property, something I'll talk about in much more depth later in the book. In fact, I'll give you my own personal due diligence system. Avoiding even one step in the process can cost you hundreds of thousands, if not millions, of dollars after you have purchased your property.

The other major thing to look for in bad management is cooked books. You probably know what cooked books are, and if you don't it's a good thing you didn't work for Enron. Believe it or not there are sellers out there that will use accounting methods to make their properties look like they produced much more income and performed much better operationally than they really did.

Why are cooked books such a big deal? Because the value of an asset is based solely on its net operating income. I had a colleague who, unfortunately, fell victim to improper accounting on a deal that he acquired. In this instance, the financials that the seller provided to the buyer reflected much higher rents than what were actually being collected—to the tune of over $102,000 per year. This oversight ended up costing my colleague greatly. Here is a chart that shows the difference in value in my colleague's asset based on the actual net operating income of the property and the NOI on the seller-provided financials:

	Actual	**"Cooked"**	
NOI	$900,000	$1,002,000	**Loss**
Capitalization Rate	6%	6%	
Purchase Price	$15,000,000	$16,700,000	$1,700,000

Can you see the power of NOI based on the chart above? Think about it, one small shift in the rents created a $1,700,000 problem for the buyer. Unfortunately this could have been avoided by a simple audit of the property files. My colleague's lack of proper due diligence ended up costing him millions in value.

Chapter 5

Key Indicators
for Success

In the previous chapter I talked about the negative factors you should look out for when purchasing an apartment building. In this section I'm going to share with you some of the key indicators that I look for when I'm beginning a search for a new property to acquire. By looking for these key indicators you will be able to weed out 90 percent of the properties that *will* waste your time, and focus on the other 10 percent that *may* waste your time. That is an exaggeration, of course, but the business of finding a solid deal is very hit or miss. Recognize that it will take time and you will run into many dead ends. But also recognize that by knowing some key indicators up front, you will greatly reduce the time spent chasing deals that don't make financial sense.

The Market

Before you look for the building, look for the market. A big mistake a lot of new investors make is that they are looking for a particular type of building rather than looking for a particular type of market. Your instincts might tell you to purchase your first apartment building in your own backyard. But this line of thinking supposes that just because you live somewhere you will be able to know the area better. While this may be true, whether you live five minutes from a market or 500 miles from a market doesn't make a substantial difference in your knowledge of that market. If you don't believe me, then tell me this: What is the average occupancy of the south part of your city?

Having a true understanding of a market takes some in-depth research. I live in Phoenix, and I operate properties in Phoenix. But I don't assume I have the knowledge I need off the top of my head to make an informed decision when it comes to acquiring a property in my hometown. Markets are constantly changing. What may have been the case a year ago could be completely different today. It would be foolish to assume that year-old information would be of use in evaluating property today.

All this is to say that when looking for an investment property don't fall into the trap of backyard sales. Do some substantial research and find a market that will allow for an incredible deal. The beauty is you don't have to settle for your hometown. If it's a horrible apartment market, go somewhere else. You will have the property professionally managed anyway. All they need from you is an address to send the checks to.

I've hired other management companies many times. As I mentioned previously, my company closed on the property in Oklahoma City. We had never been there, and we had never invested or operated there. What we did know is that Oklahoma City was a solid apartment market with affordable properties. That was all we needed to set us off on an expansive research mission. We ended up finding a great building at the perfect price. Many people are surprised to find that my company doesn't manage the building. In fact, I hired a company much like mine that would be considered a competitor if it were located in Phoenix. But it was a terrific decision. I get all the money and none of the headache. The following are some things that you should look for when seeking a perfect market for your next investment.

CYCLES

Ever hear the cliché that real estate markets are cyclical? Well, sometimes clichés exist because they are true. That is certainly the case when it comes to this one. Real estate markets will have their peaks and valleys—some more extreme than others. The key for you as an investor is to be able to recognize those cycles and to buy in the valleys. It is the simple concept of—are you ready for another cliché?—buy low and sell high. How do you know when a market is in the valley? That's a good question. Here's the answer.

First off, there are some valleys that you don't want to buy in. What I mean is that there are markets that are just beginning to fall. The key is to find a market that is at its lowest point, find the right property, and then ride the wave all the way to the top again. This is my tried-and-true method. I've been able to amass huge amounts of profit by purchasing properties this way. The reasons are fairly obvious. Since the value of a real estate asset is based on its NOI, you can find the best deals in a market where rents are low, vacancies are high, and concessions are present. But a property like that is only a good deal if the market is ready to pick up again—that occupancy will get better and rents will rise. When you find an investment in a market like that, you will be able to add value to your property just by riding the wave of the market.

A couple of years ago, Las Vegas was a perfect market. With this in mind I purchased two buildings in the city in 2004. We definitely bought at the right time; rents and occupancy have been on the rise ever since.

When we were purchasing our buildings in the beginning of 2004, we were purchasing at just the right time. The market had been flat for a couple of years, and experienced negative growth because of a downturn in tourism after 9/11. Those lean years had caused a lot of landlords to just want to get out. Consequently, we were able to purchase the buildings based on the operational value. At the time, properties were experiencing high vacancy and high rental concessions or incentives. When we were looking to invest in the Las Vegas apartment market, there were a number of indicators we felt boded well for the rental market in the coming years. These are the same indicators you should look for when you are beginning the search for your investment market.

POPULATION AND EMPLOYMENT GROWTH

The number one indicator that a market is ready to explode is to look at its population and employment growth statistics, which are available on the Internet and through public information services, like the U.S. Census Bureau, and are projected by a number of sources. The simple fact of the matter is that growth will beget growth. When you have a lot of jobs being formed in a market, a lot of people move there to fill them. Those people will need places to live. When moving to a new city, even those that can afford to purchase a house will often rent for a period of time before purchasing a home, and a certain percentage will always rent. Ideally, rapid employment and population growth create pressure on both vacancies and rents, since there is no way for the supply of apartments to keep up with demand.

The above indicators attracted us most to the Las Vegas marketplace. We knew that it was a city that was expected to see some very strong growth in both the employment and population segments. Additionally, we knew that most of the jobs created were going to be in the service industry through casinos. By doing a little research, we knew that the largest expansion of the Las Vegas Strip in history was going to happen over the next decade. A number of casinos were in development and it was estimated that over the next several years over 35,000 new hotel rooms would come on-line. This would be a major boost to the Las Vegas economy with future employment and population growth. This would also provide upward pressure on the existing supply of for-sale and rental housing. We knew that the demographics in Las Vegas had been traditionally strong, and that they were just coming out of a rough patch in employment growth.

Now let's compare employment and population growth with apartment rent. Here is a chart comparing the statistics:

Las Vegas—Population, Employment, and Rent Growth

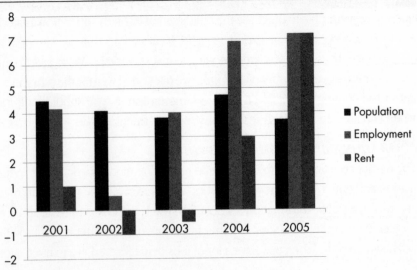

Source: Don Hendricks, Hendricks & Partners

As you can see, there is a fairly coherent pattern connecting employment and job growth with rental growth. Notice that 2002 was the worst year for Las Vegas employment growth. It is also the worst year for rents. The decline in employment growth and population growth from previous years caused rents to drop by one percent. By 2003, however, employment growth was up again. And, as expected, rents did not climb immediately. The reason is that it will always take a little more time for rents to readjust to changing market conditions because leases last from six months to a year, and rents cannot be raised until the leases expire. But once we began to see the positive trends in employment and population we were confident that rent growth would follow and began searching for properties to purchase in early 2003.

Looking at our graph, it's apparent that the market experienced an amazing run in both job and population growth in 2003 and in the years following. It culminated in 2005 with an astounding 7 percent gain in job and rental growth. Just think, the national average for job growth is generally around 1.5 percent. Between the time we had purchased the building and the end of 2005, rents had increased by 3 percent in 2004 and 7 percent in 2005. Using simple math, let me show you what kind of impact rent growth can have on the value of a $10 million building.

Rent Growth		NOI	Cap Rate	Asset Value
	2003	$600,000	6%	$10,000,000
3%	2004	$618,000	6%	$10,300,000
7%	2005	$661,260	6%	$11,021,000
			Total	$1,021,000

As you can see from the chart, over $1 million was added in value just by understanding the power of cycles in real estate and knowing the right time to buy.

One thing you may be thinking to yourself is that the negative rent growth in 2002 is a little odd since the population growth was still around 4 percent. There is another factor besides employment and population growth that determines negative rent growth: In 2002 there was a significant amount of new construction, which added a large number of multifamily units to the market.

SUPPLY AND DEMAND

In Las Vegas there was a huge amount of demand for apartments precisely because of the population and employment growth. At the same period of time land prices and construction costs were very low. In order to meet the demand, developers rushed to build multifamily buildings. In the process, several thousand more units were built than were needed. Those units had to be absorbed. Absorption is when demand catches up with supply. This can take years to happen—especially in markets where the population and job growth are slow or even negative.

Because there were so many units on the market and not enough renters to fill them, rents were decreased significantly in an effort to keep occupancy high. Additionally, concessions like one month of free rent were being offered in order to lure prospective renters away from other communities. You've heard of a buyer's market—well this was definitely a renter's market. The combination of these efforts decreased the net operating income of these properties and consequently decreased their value.

In Las Vegas, we knew that population and job growth would continue to remain strong and that once the excess apartment inventory wasn't as big of a problem, rents would rise again. There was also one other factor that we knew would bode well for the near future rental market—condominium conversions and the price of housing.

The price of housing in Las Vegas rose at unbelievable levels over 2004 and 2005. Appreciation levels ranged from 20 to 50 percent in some areas. There was no way that the income level of the city's residents could catch up with the rising price of housing. Consequently, many people were beginning to be priced out of the market. They couldn't afford to purchase a home because their salaries were not growing at the same pace as the cost of housing. Furthermore, the people who were moving into the city were coming to take advantage of the job growth, but those jobs didn't pay enough to allow them to purchase a home. They had to rent. There was a shortage of affordable housing.

In an effort to meet the demand for affordable housing, many investors and developers swooped into town. Taking advantage of the decreased value of multifamily housing, they purchased apartment buildings in order to convert them to condominiums. Maybe you've heard of condominium conversions.

They've been prevalent in every real estate cycle. Basically a condominium conversion is exactly what it sounds like. A developer purchases an apartment building, works with the city to change the legal status of the building from an apartment to condominium, and then sells the units to individual buyers.

It's estimated that over 10,000 units in Las Vegas were taken off the rental market for condominium conversion purposes between 2003 and 2005. That's definitely one way to further help reduce vacancies and increase rents! Take a look at the graph on supply and demand.

Las Vegas—Multifamily—Supply and Demand

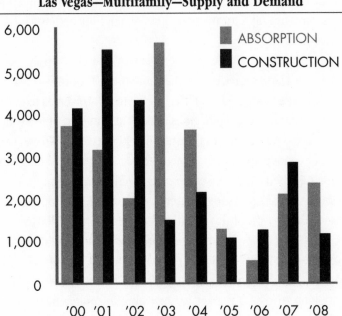

Source: Don Hendricks, Hendricks & Partners

Do you see the correction between construction in 2001 and absorption in 2003? That is a direct result of condominium conversions. We had been paying attention to the market trends by reading reports of sales activities in Las Vegas. We knew what was coming, and we knew that if we purchased an apartment building at the right time, we would be able capitalize on this market trend.

What the condominium conversion craze in Las Vegas created was a situation that I refer to as "negative apartment growth." That may sound like a bad thing, but it isn't if you are a landlord. According to the Southern Nevada Multifamily Association, almost 11,000 units were removed from the market due to the condominium conversions.

While thousands of new residents needing an affordable place to live were moving into the city, many of the affordable rental units were being removed from the market. The idea was of course to make the condominiums an affordable alternative purchase option to a house, but the appreciation in the Las Vegas market caused the price of many of the condominium conversion units to become too high for many people. Again, they had nowhere to turn but to rental housing.

Unfortunately for developers, when growth exceeds supply, the cost of construction and land skyrockets at the same time. That meant that as thousands of units were being pulled off the market to be converted to condominiums, there were no replacement units being built. In fact, only a total of 600 units were built to replace the diminished inventory of 11,000 over two years. That caused negative apartment growth: fewer apartments being built than were being absorbed. This caused a reversal of the preceding years' trends, and now instead of supply being greater than demand, the opposite was true. This caused rents to shoot through the roof beginning in 2004. By the first quarter of 2005, the rate of apartment rent growth had spiked to over 8 percent, according to M/PF YieldStar.

I know that I've thrown in a lot of statistics in order to make my point: When you are looking to pick a market for investing in multifamily housing, you should pick a market that is in the valley, not at its peak, when it comes to employment growth, population growth, and supply and demand. Today the buildings that we purchased are renting at rates 10 to 12 percent higher than when we purchased them. Additionally, we don't have to offer any concessions to renters and our occupancy rate is in the mid-90 percent. I bet the owners who bailed because of a couple bad years wish they had held on. I'm glad they didn't because their lack of foresight has greatly benefited our investors.

BARRIERS TO GROWTH
Besides employment growth, population growth, and demand—what I believe to be the top three indicators of a good market—there are some other

indicators that you should look for that can be a great benefit to you as an investor. I'm speaking of barriers to growth, geographically or self-imposed, such as urban growth boundaries.

A barrier to growth is anything that would prevent further development of apartment buildings in a certain area. There are many things that can contribute to this:

- Submarkets that are fully built out or developed
- Government-protected land
- City boundaries
- Zoning changes
- Natural formations such as mountain ranges or bodies of water

Las Vegas is a good example of a market with barriers to growth. The city is almost completely built out, meaning that it cannot expand further into the desert such as a city like Phoenix can. The reason is that on one side Las Vegas is surrounded by a mountain range, and on the others it is surrounded by federally protected land. The federal government has set aside 400,000 acres that cannot be developed because of the desert tortoise—a near extinct terrapin that has been placed under endangered species protection. If there were any reason to be an environmentalist, this would be one. If the preserved land were to be released for development, the price of real estate could tumble due to oversupply, and as I'm sure you've guessed the rental market would suffer greatly as the price of housing came down, and more apartments were added to the supply.

Since the city can no longer build outward, developers have been forced to build on the already scarce land in the city's boundaries. This has led to high land values since there is not nearly enough land to meet the demand. The term "Manhattanization" has been coined to describe the changes happening in the Las Vegas real estate market. Instead of traditional garden-style apartments—properties with outdoor entrances that are two to three stories high and spread over large lots—being built, there's been a huge influx of mid- and high-rise apartment and condominium buildings. In essence, the city is building up since it cannot build out.

If you know anything about the Manhattan real estate market, you know what can happen to a geographic area that has no choice but to build up.

Manhattan is an island that has practically no land left to build on. Tall buildings are expensive to build and expensive to operate. Affordability goes out the window. All of this is caused by a city's barriers to growth. The inability to find new land will inevitably lead to higher and higher buildings—and higher and higher real estate values. In fact, the most expensive high-rise development in the United States is being built in Las Vegas as I write this. The total projected cost: $7 billion. To put that in perspective, if the project were a person, it would be one of the fifty richest people in the United States—and that doesn't even include cost overruns!

Some cities have instituted their own legislated versions of barriers to growth. These are commonly called urban growth boundaries. There are a variety of reasons why a city will enact an urban growth boundary, and they can be controversial. Portland, Oregon, for instance, did it intentionally in order to counteract suburban sprawl. In Flagstaff, they have instituted an urban growth boundary in order to preserve the natural beauty of the land surrounding the city. The municipality is located in a gorgeous mountain setting that is ringed by state parks and miles upon miles of hiking trails. Since the city depends on tourism as its main economic source, they want to preserve as much of the natural land as possible. No matter the reasoning behind it, there is little doubt that urban growth boundaries contribute to rising hosing costs. More than three-quarters of the people living in the Flagstaff area say the cost of living is unaffordable—with housing as the number one concern.

Portland enacted its urban growth boundary in the 1970s. Since then, housing costs have been on the rise. Today, Portland is considered one of the ten least affordable housing markets in the country. The price of housing in the Portland metropolitan area has appreciated 56.6 percent over the last five years alone. This has created an affordable housing shortage that has helped to bolster the Portland apartment market. In 2006, apartment rents rose in Portland by 6 percent.

Though they are not a sure sign of a great rental market, barriers to growth and urban growth boundaries are something that you should keep an eye on when looking at a potential market. Coupled with the other indicators that I've talked about in this section, they can be a potent catalyst to growth.

URBAN RENEWAL

Another indicator to look for when evaluating a market is urban renewal. This is a trend that has been catching on more and more across the nation. Basically, urban renewal is an effort to reestablish cities' downtown areas as thriving civic centers where people live, work, and play. There are a number of cities that are actively renewing their urban areas. Portland, for instance, enacted its urban growth boundary specifically to encourage people to move into the city center rather than out. Other cities that have undertaken major urban renewal projects are Austin, Texas, and Seattle, Washington.

Why is this important? In areas where urban renewal is just beginning, there are huge opportunities to purchase real estate at an exceptional value. Once an urban area starts to realize a surge in population, the price of housing in that area soars. I saw this many years ago in Vancouver, British Columbia.

I was on vacation there and asked what area I could visit that was up and coming. A majority of the residents told me that Yaletown was the hippest place to be—and they were right. You probably have been to places like this. The area was comprised of old warehouses that had been purchased and re-developed into cool shops and restaurants. Entrepreneurial individuals were taking advantage of zoning changes in the city to purchase buildings cheaply and creating a young, trendy neighborhood in the process.

The neighborhood is located right on the water. While I was walking around, I was amazed by the fact that there were high-rise condominiums right on the waterfront that were selling for $100,000—Canadian! At the time the exchange rate was 75 percent. That meant with U.S. currency I could have purchased a high-rise condominium for $75,000. Unfortunately, I didn't. Today those same condominiums sell for $350,000 and Yaletown is the spot to be. An investment in a condominium in Yaletown back then would have been a great move, but purchasing an apartment building would have been an even better one. Everyone wants to live there but can't afford to. They have to rent because according to Bizmapbc.com, housing prices in the neighborhood average over $590,000—significantly higher than Vancouver's average housing price of $364,033. In fact over 98 percent of all dwellings in Yaletown are apartments.

In most areas where urban renewal is happening, a majority of the residents that move into the city center are younger individuals who are not able to purchase housing. Rentals are the major source of housing. It is always a good idea to check into these types of areas—you might be able to find a screaming deal.

Chapter 6

The Next Top Ten Markets to Watch

I know what you're thinking, "Thanks for all this theory, now how about some application?" In this chapter we'll take the indicators for success that I talked about in the previous chapter and apply them. I'm going to give you my personal top ten list of multifamily markets to watch. I'm not a prophet, so I can't guarantee that these markets will perform well. What I can do is show you some positive patterns that will help you make an informed decision on where you want to invest. What you do with the patterns is up to you.

#1. Seattle

Seattle has often been overlooked in recent years as a powerhouse multifamily market, but experts are now beginning to see the light. There are a couple of very strong indicators that get me excited about this market in the coming years. We'll call them the usual suspects: affordable housing, job growth, and supply issues.

Affordable housing is and will continue to be a huge issue in the Seattle metropolitan area. Over the last seven years the median housing price in the city has skyrocketed by over 80 percent. Prices have gone up from $250,000 to over $420,000. And the growth is not expected to stop anytime soon. Over the last couple of years, the metropolitan area has seen year-over-year growth in the double digits—while most of the country was experiencing little or no growth. Many experts predict that the price of housing will continue to grow in the low teens over the next few years and that it may be the next huge coastal growth market, much like San Francisco.

So what does this mean for the multifamily investor? The increase in housing prices has outpaced income growth, and that means that more and more people won't be able to purchase a house and will have to rent an apartment instead. What makes the significant growth in housing so exciting is that the city is also experiencing solid job and population growth at the same time.

Everyone knows that Boeing and Microsoft are the two major employers in Seattle, and they will be the driving force of continued job growth in the city. It is expected that over the next two years, more than 75,000 jobs will be created in the city. This will continue to be a strain on the housing market and will push the price of single-family houses out of reach for most individuals. Boeing announced record contracts and will have plenty of employment opportunites over the next few years. Many of these jobs are in manufacturing and simply do not pay enough to allow for the average family to purchase a home. This is good news for multifamily investors because a majority will opt to rent. Additionally, Microsoft is gearing up to expand its already gargantuan corporate campus by fourteen buildings in the next three years. The expansion will cost over $1 billion and will create over 12,000 jobs. All this job growth will spur population growth as people move into the area to take advantage of the employment opportunities.

The growth in jobs and population coupled with extremely unaffordable housing will create a big demand for rental housing. According to Hendricks & Partners, a prominent brokerage firm, demand for apartments will dramatically outpace the ability of developers to construct them. In the next couple of years, there will be demand for two and a half apartments for every one apartment that is built. The chart on the next page shows what the supply and demand for the market is projected to look like. As you can see, rents will be pushed higher and will definitely create low vacancy. That's a winning combination in any market.

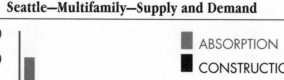

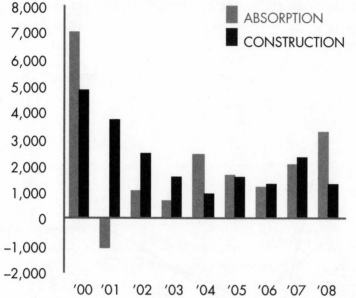

Seattle—Multifamily—Supply and Demand

Source: Don Hendricks, Hendricks & Partners

As of right now, the rents and occupancies in the Seattle market have stabilized after some significant gains since 2002, but the continued affordability issues and the coming job growth will cause the apartment investments to realize higher rents and full occupancies for the foreseeable future.

#2. San Francisco

The San Francisco apartment market is just now coming out of a significant decrease in rents that occurred after the technology market imploded. The reduction in employment was disastrous for the rental market as rents seemed to drop at the same rate as jobs—that is, like flies. The graph, created from statistics gathered by Hendricks & Partners, shows the direct correlation between the two phenomena. While occupancies remained steady throughout the period after the tech bubble burst—the average price for a house in San Francisco is over $800,000—you can see how the reduction in employment drastically affected what the owners were able to charge for an apartment. Well, thankfully that time has passed. San Francisco is finally experiencing postive gains in the employment sector, and a renaissance in the technology sector as well as expansion in manufacturing and construction jobs are the driving forces.

San Francisco—Jobs and Rental Growth

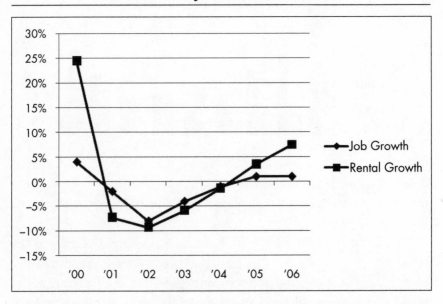

San Francisco tops the Urban Land Institute's (ULI) list of markets to watch as well. According to their well-produced report, *Emerging Trends in Real Estate,* the city is "back from the dead" and "making a tremendous surge." All experts in the study recommend investing in the city's multifamily market. San Francisco's position as a major global economic intersection and the reenergized technology market are the major reasons cited. But also not to be overlooked is San Francisco's appeal to younger individuals who are longing for an urban metropolitan area that provides localized neighborhoods where they can work, play, shop, and live.

As I wrote earlier in the book, the majority of households under the age of twenty-nine rent rather than own. As cities like San Francisco continue to attract younger and younger residents to their vibrant urban centers, the gap between residents and affordable housing will continue to increase. This will play a major factor in the San Francisco rental market as a steady stream of new residents will have no option other than to rent an apartment.

Another excellent aspect to the San Francisco rental market is the limited amount of land that is available to develop. This has caused land values to skyrocket, and this, coupled with very high material and construction costs, has deterred new apartment construction. Lack of new inventory in the face of steady employment and population growth is going to make for a very favorable rental market in the coming years. San Francisco is a sure bet.

#3. Los Angeles Metropolitan Area

As the second largest metropolitan area in the nation and the entertainment mecca of the world, Los Angeles has always been attractive for those looking for a new hometown. While the employment and job growth in L.A. are predicted to remain roughly at the same level as that of the rest of the nation, there are some indicators that stand to make Los Angeles—especially South Los Angeles—one of the top markets to watch in the coming years.

Probably the biggest reason is that South Los Angeles County won't be building any new apartments in the next couple of years. That means that even modest population growth will put a strain on the existing apartment inventory, and there will be more demand than supply in the market, causing rents to grow and vacancies to decrease.

Additionally, Los Angeles housing prices continue to rise in a market that is already one of the most unaffordable in the nation. The average housing price in the metropolitan area is well above $550,000. To put that in perspective, here is the money it would take to purchase a house at the average price in Los Angeles versus the monthly rental payment for the same house:

Purchase Price	$ 550,000
Down Payment (20%)	$ 110,000
Monthly Mortgage Payment (6.5% Interest Only)	$ 2,380
Average Rental Payment	$ 1,300

I don't know about you, but most people can't afford a $2,380 a month mortgage payment. That doesn't even take into account taxes and insurance. The larger the gap is between mortgage rates and rental rates, the better for a landlord. Compare the average monthly mortgage payment of $2,380 with the average monthly rental rate of $1,300 and you'll see why more and more people are turning to rental housing rather than purchasing. In fact, of the 22,000 people that are projected to move to L.A. in the near future, 25 percent will be between the prime renting ages of eighteen and thirty-four, according to Sperry Van Ness, a commercial real estate firm. This trend has already started as home sales in the L.A. area have decreased significantly from previous years.

Los Angeles is also high on my list because of the city's efforts to begin developing a vibrant downtown scene—something it has never had and that has been considered a huge detriment to the city. A significant development in this renaissance came in 1999 when the city passed an ordinance making it easier for developers to purchase abandoned buildings and turn them into lofts and luxury apartment buildings. Workers tired of the horrendously bad traffic and two-hour commutes are now moving into the downtown corridor to live in these new apartments. The population of the downtown area has seen increases of over 20 percent in the last couple years, and this kind of growth is expected to continue for at least the next year. Money is pouring into the downtown sector, and there are new skyscrapers, parks, and retail centers in the works. The time is now to acquire in this up-and-coming area.

#4. Las Vegas

As I discussed earlier, Las Vegas is a stellar rental market because of its incredible job and population growth as well as its barriers to growth, which have created a shortage of affordable land to develop. Make no doubt about it, Las Vegas will continue to develop into an economic powerhouse when it comes to the multifamily industry.

The number one factor that makes Las Vegas a market to watch is its employment and population growth. The city has consistently been in the top five in the nation in both categories and is showing no signs of slowing. The city is expected to add thousands of new employment opportunities, mostly in the service and construction industries, which are expected to draw over 50,000 new residents next year, according to Sperry Van Ness.

Other developments in the city are very attractive for future employment and population growth as well. Remember the $7 billion City Center project I told you about earlier? It is estimated that when that project is complete in a couple years, it will create over 35,000 jobs alone. The development will be spread over forty-four acres and will be comprised of 2,800 condominiums, 4,000 hotel rooms, a casino, and a huge shopping center. That is just one project. There are dozens of high-rise buildings in the works. By some estimates, there is $10 billion in investments going into revitalizing the downtown area over the next five years, all of which will create jobs in both the service and construction industries. Overall there doesn't appear to be many high-salary jobs on the horizon. That's good news for landlords in a market where the cost of housing is increasingly unaffordable. All those people with modest incomes will need somewhere reasonably priced to live.

The rising cost of housing is no secret in Las Vegas. The median housing price is over $340,000, which prices most of the service-oriented workers out of the market. After all, working the tables at a casino may be glamorous, but it certainly doesn't pay well. While the market has hit a recent bump in the road and won't see appreciation at the same levels as it has in the recent past, housing prices are expected to keep rising in the long term, due to the mountains and government land that surround the city. There just isn't any more land to build out on. That will continue to cause the price of land to rise, and housing along with it.

Because of the nature of the workforce in Las Vegas, the rental market is poised to have continued strong growth. Rents are projected to rise at 4 to 5 percent per year for the foreseeable future, and the limited supply of apartments will cause vacancies to shrink and concessions to disappear.

#5. Austin

Austin, Texas, is an often overlooked market for many because it is not a major metropolitan area like some of the other cities on this list. The city, however, is considered to be at the top of the list when it comes to smaller rental markets according to the Urban Land Institute, and I couldn't agree more.

Austin is home to the University of Texas, one of the largest universities in the country. But the city is more than just a college town. It is one of the major centers for technology firms, including Dell, Qualcomm, and Intel, and Austin has consistently been one of the top job-growth markets in the United States.

It's not just jobs that are growing in Austin. The population is skyrocketing as well. The city is expected to become the third largest in Texas within the decade. No doubt about it, Austin is definitely on the upswing from an economic valley that started in 2002.

Major development is taking place in the city. A couple of large-scale shopping centers are in the works, and Marriott and W hotels are scheduled to build in the revitalized downtown area. The city is working hard to create a vibrant downtown area by offering financial incentives to developers. Mid-to high-rise apartment buildings with retail shops like restaurants and boutiques are being built throughout the downtown area, and scores of young people are moving into the area to take advantage of the hip and active lifestyle.

Housing prices in Austin are on the rise, too. Over the last couple of years, housing prices have risen by 7 to 8 percent. The influx of residents from other areas taking advantage of the thriving job market is creating ample demand for apartment housing, as is the student population—50,000 of whom live off-campus.

Another key advantage that Austin has over other markets is its affordability for the multifamily investor. Average price per unit for apartment buildings in Austin is below the levels in other powerhouse markets. Rents are more than able to sustain Austin's prices, making many potential acquisitions well-performing assets when it comes to cash flow. And rents are only expected to rise.

More good news for multifamily investors interested in the Austin market is that the majority of those moving into the city are projected to be thirty-five years or younger, and the median age in Austin is thirty-one and a half. As I've mentioned before, those are the prime renting years for most people. As more and more young people move into Austin to take advantage of its culture and job growth, the multifamily industry will flourish.

#6. Denver

I think that the Urban Land Institute sums up the Denver market best when they say, "Denver is in the sweet spot of an upcycle—good absorption and increasing rents." The city is part of ULI's list of markets to watch and for good reason. In the past the market has suffered greatly from too many apartments being constructed and not enough demand. Times, however, are changing in the Mile High City. Take a look at the projected absorption in the coming years, according to Hendricks & Partners. When looking at this graph, it becomes pretty obvious that there will be a huge need for more multifamily housing in the next couple of years. Unfortunately, or fortunately, depending on your perspective, there will not be enough construction to meet demand. You know what that means—occupancies will go up and then rents will increase.

Denver—Multifamily—Supply and Demand

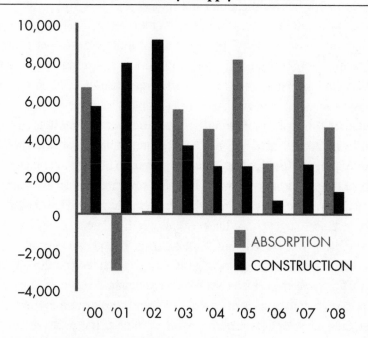

Source: Don Hendricks, Hendricks & Partners

The economic future of Denver looks bright, too. Job growth is expected to rise at roughly 2 to 3 percent over the next couple of years, and more than one million people are expected to flood the city in the next twenty years. In order to accommodate the expected population influx, the city is making huge strides in developing a mass transportation system. The city has six new lines in the works that will cover 120 miles throughout the city. All the railroad lines will move into the downtown area—the largest concentration of employment in the city. There are plans to make the already burgeoning downtown a vital and vibrant city center. If you are planning on investing in the Denver market, you would do well to try to purchase properties that will be located near these rail lines. Any property that is will almost certainly increase in value.

The new transportation system will be a plus for the residents in the city, and there is hope that once the system is in place, more and more companies will be enticed to relocate to the city or set up satellite offices. This could be a huge shot in the arm for the employment sector in the city and would of course greatly benefit the multifamily industry.

#7. *Tucson*

Tucson is often overshadowed by its much larger neighbor Phoenix, but this small city is a hidden gem when it comes to multifamily investment. The city, home to the University of Arizona, has traditionally been considered a large college town, but Tucson is now becoming a metropolitan area in its own right as both population and job growth are expected to be high in coming years.

Thanks to California's restricting business taxes, many businesses are relocating to Tucson because of its favorable business climate and lower cost of living. For instance, Target chose Tucson for its new fulfillment center over seven other sites they were considering. A spokesman for Target said that they chose Tucson because of its strategic location and the fact that it's a progressive community with a skilled workforce. The center will provide over 900 jobs alone.

A favorable climate, a lower cost of living, and employment opportunities are also creating strong population growth in the city. It is predicted that the population of Tucson will surpass one million by 2010.

What is exciting to me about the Tucson rental market is that despite the strong employment and population growth, construction of new apartments will be very low. Here is the projected absorption and construction for the coming years according to a Hendricks & Partners forecast:

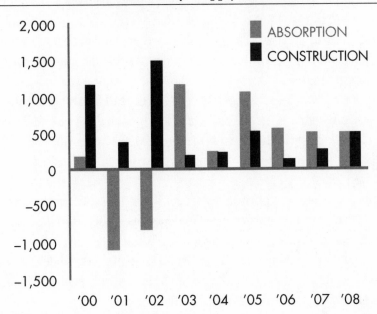

Tucson—Multifamily—Supply and Demand

Source: Don Hendricks, Hendricks & Partners

Following the pattern I've shown you many times in this book, the continued strong population and employment growth in Tucson will create higher demand for apartment housing with limited supply coming. That is music to investors' ears. Landlords will be able to increase rents and concessions should become a thing of the past in the market as occupancies rise. With its solid demographics, Tucson looks set to be a strong rental market for years to come.

#8. *Phoenix*

Phoenix is my hometown, so naturally you should have expected it to end up on my list of markets to watch! But that's not the only reason. Phoenix continues to be an incredible market to invest in due to its strong employment opportunities and population growth. The Phoenix metropolitan area is one of the fastest growing markets in the entire country, and there is no sign of its stopping.

The biggest draws for people coming to Phoenix are lower cost of living, job opportunities, and quality of living. We are the Valley of the Sun after all. It's estimated by the U.S. Census Bureau that Arizona will actually double its population by the year 2030 to 5.6 million people. Phoenix has consistently outpaced national job growth by double digits. It's not uncommon to hear of the population growing by over 100,000 people in a given year.

The job forecast for Phoenix is very good, too. The city has been in the top three when it comes to job growth over the last couple of years. Many companies are relocating to the area due to more favorable tax environments than other states, such as California, causing the job market to rise steadily over the past seven years.

Phoenix would be higher on my list if it weren't for the coming problem with oversupply. The influx of new residents has caused developers to increase apartment construction activity and it is estimated that supply will be slightly higher than demand over the next couple of years. While this won't have a huge negative impact on the market, rents aren't expected to increase at the same stellar percentages that they have been.

Besides new construction, the supply of rental units will be influenced by what real estate junkies call the "shadow market." Shadow market is a buzzword that simply means rental supply that is not comprised of traditional apartment buildings. In the case of Phoenix, these will be single-family homes and condominiums that were purchased by investors.

A couple of years ago the condominium conversion craze in Phoenix was at its peak. Some 11,000 apartment units were taken off the market. This has been a dampener for the market since there is no way to gauge how many of those units were sold to people who were going to own and live in them, or to investors who were going to rent them out.

Despite the reservations I have about the market regarding oversupply, I feel confident that Phoenix will be an awesome rental market to invest in if you find the right opportunity. Its rock-solid job and employment growth can't be ignored and will continue to spur huge demand for apartment rental units as, again, affordability is an issue.

According to the U.S. Census Bureau, 22 percent of the Arizona population is under thirty-four years of age. Those numbers are expected to hold steady or grow. As the price of housing continues to escalate, many of those people will be priced out of the housing market. That will allow landlords to increase rents and occupancies.

One additional factor that will be a positive for multifamily owners in the Phoenix market is the disastrously horrible traffic patterns. In the inner city where the majority of jobs are located, the land is pretty much built out. The highest home values are in these areas. While there is plenty of land in the valley for building, developers increasingly have to build further and further out to provide affordable housing. This urban sprawl is creating longer and longer commutes as the huge population growth is more than outpacing the ability of the state to create more roads. I think that you will see a growing trend of people—young people especially—who will opt out of home ownership in order to rent closer to their work centers.

#9. Boise

Boise, Idaho, is another up-and-coming small metropolitan area that many investors haven't paid any attention to. With a population of over 560,000, Boise is experiencing strong population growth of 3 to 4 percent per year. What is even more impressive, however, is the rate at which employment is growing: 5 to 6 percent in recent years. Most growth has been and will be focused in the construction trade, transportation, and public administration.

All of this growth is creating an upward pressure on the price of housing, and while the rest of the country has been experiencing sluggish growth in their housing markets, Boise is performing at the top of its game, and is expected to weather the national downturn well. The continued growth in the city is expected to sustain home price increases in the coming years, and the multifamily market in the city is just now beginning to recover from a period of very poor performance.

Additionally, limited construction will continue to help the rental market remain tight. Rents are expected to rise at close to 4 percent per year over the coming years and vacancies are expected to be very low, hovering between 4 and 5 percent. This will be due primarily to the rising cost of housing and the limited amount of new apartment inventory that is scheduled to be constructed.

The downside to the Boise market? Pricing. Boise would be much higher on my list if there was a larger amount of inventory available at affordable pricing. Current owners have gotten a little greedy and are basing selling prices on projected rental market performance rather than on actual performance. There are still good deals to be had in Boise, but make sure to be careful and base your offer on realistic numbers and not market projections. It remains to be seen how many transactions will take place in large multifamily acquisitions. If owners are unable to find buyers at the current pricing, there may be a small window of opportunity to cash in on a value purchase before the market really takes off.

#10. Albuquerque

With a population of over 820,000, Albuquerque, New Mexico, is on the verge of surpassing the one million resident mark and becoming a major metropolitan area. The city is experiencing a renaissance of sorts as both employment and population growth are strong, hovering around 3 percent, and the median price of housing is growing at a brisk pace.

Recently, the median housing price surpassed the $200,000 mark in Albuquerque for the first time. The market is predicted to continue to lead the nation in single-family home appreciation. Pricing is expected to continue rising over the coming years due to an influx of new residents seeking to take advantage of the low cost of living, the quality of life, and the thriving job market.

Employment growth is expected to remain in the 2.5 to 3 percent range for the foreseeable future with an up-and-coming entertainment industry, in addition to manufacturing, and high-tech. The continual growth of the housing market should price a good number of new residents coming to the city to take advantage of the job growth out of the ownership market and that will make for a very competitive rental market. Here is what *New Mexico Business Weekly* had to say about the future of the apartment market: "Rents should go up, concessions to residents should cease and building values will increase significantly."

The reason is fairly simple: Albuquerque is a barrier-to-growth market because there currently is a significant shortage of land zoned for multifamily. That means there will be very little supply to meet the growing demand for apartments in the future, and absorption is predicted to outpace supply in the coming years.

Many experts feel that the combination of all these factors will make Albuquerque one of the hottest multifamily markets in a few years, and large multifamily companies are just now beginning to notice the market. For now, the buildings still can be bought at a very reasonable price and it appears that the market is getting ready to take off.

Do Your Research!

Whether you choose to invest in the markets I've listed above or another market, you should always do your homework. Never take what "experts" say as gospel. Market conditions are dynamic. That means that they can change at the drop of a hat, depending on any number of variables. As I always say, trust but verify.

Remember, "top ten" doesn't necessarily mean "top choice." If you limit yourself to markets that "experts," have identified as top markets, you will miss out on a lot of deals. In the end, there are thousands of markets to choose from when looking to invest in multifamily properties. That means that even if a market isn't "top ten" material, it can still be a great market to invest in—especially if you find the right deal.

By way of example, I've talked a bit about my Oklahoma City acquisition in this book. One reason is that it is my most recent investment, but the other is because it is an example of a great deal. The Oklahoma City apartment market is a solid market and the demographics of the city are looking better and better all the time. Job growth is high and population growth is steady. I invested there because a broker package on the property I eventually ended up buying piqued my interest. The more I began to research the market, the more I was interested. The property was affordable and had great potential to provide returns. There is nothing exciting, per se, about the Oklahoma City market like there is about some of the other markets I mentioned, but it is a solid market and I was presented with a great deal. Through research and keeping your eyes open, you, too, will be able to find great deals whether they are in a "top ten" market or a different, yet solid, market such as Oklahoma City.

In my first book, *The ABC's of Real Estate Investing*, I go into detail on my system of research so I won't get too detailed here. In summary, it is comprised of three levels:

Level 1 Research: This can be done easily from the comfort of your own home. Spend a good deal of time researching all the economic details you possibly can about a market you are interested in. I'm talking about everything from median home prices to proposed developments that might impact the multifamily market. This is the time to just simply collect any and all data you can. You will be able to verify it later.

Level 2 Research: This is the time when you can hit the ground running. You travel to your proposed market and meet with area experts. In this level of research you begin to formulate your team, many of whom will confirm your data from level 1 or correct it if necessary. You jam your days full of meetings, taking advantage of the knowledge of city officials, brokers, and property management companies. It's a lot of work, but a lot of fun, too.

Level 3 Research: Once you have gathered all your information and seen the market with your own eyes, you need to return home and digest all that you have learned. In level 3 research, you speak with trusted business partners and discuss your findings with them. Often they will have additional information and be able to point out things you might have missed. A second set of eyes is always a good thing in business and real estate investing.

Facts, Not Feelings

Once you have processed everything, and gone through the three levels of research, only then do you decide whether to move forward in a market. Always remember, multifamily investing is not about how you feel. It's about facts. If you find that the facts don't support what is being said, then drop the market or property and move on. When it comes to multifamily investments, investing with your feelings will only lead you to disaster, but using your head will lead you to success. If you spend the time and effort required to fully research your investment market, you will be able to find the right opportunity. Then comes the exciting part—moving forward with a purchase. For the rest of the book, I'll walk you through the process of purchasing a multifamily building from the offer to the close of escrow. In the end you'll be equipped with the knowledge to successfully find and acquire your own multifamily assets.

Chapter 7

The Purchase Process

So far we've gone over the advantages of real estate over any other investment, and the advantage of multifamily over any other real estate investment. I've shown you how to examine markets, when to purchase your multifamily investment, and explored some different strategies through my own investments. Now I will walk you through the actual purchase process by showing you the steps we took when recently acquiring our building in Oklahoma City.

Some of this information is found in my first book, *The ABC's of Real Estate Investing*. But I will expand on several topics, including one very important one: the process of due diligence. By now you know that due diligence is the period of time in a purchase process where you roll up your sleeves and investigate every aspect of a property and its operations. It is a time to flush out all the details and examine how they might affect you and the operations of the property, should you close escrow and take ownership of the property. In this chapter, I'll show you how vitally important due diligence is to the purchase process—especially in the kinds of deals we are talking about here, which are large multifamily acquisitions. But before I do that, I'll do a quick review of some of the process that leads up the due diligence period.

Offer

Don't believe hype. I've said it earlier in the book and I'm going to say it again here. Don't base your offer on anything other than the actual operations of a property. The formula is very simple:

Net Operating Income ÷ Capitalization Rate = Value

That means if you are purchasing a property based on a seller pro forma, don't believe the hype. Naturally, sellers don't have your best interest in mind. Generally any purchase price on a seller's pro forma will be based on "future" operations—whether they are obtainable or not.

My favorite trick to catch is the rent roll shuffle. When you get a marketing piece for a property, often the seller will base the projected net operating income off of a rent roll that is quite a bit different from the actual one. Take my Oklahoma property as an example. When we first received the offering package from the seller's broker, the rent roll listed was this:

FLOOR PLAN	UNIT COUNT	UNIT TYPE	SQ. FT.	MARKET RENT/MO.	RENT/SQ. FT.
A	132	1 × 1	744	$425	$0.57
B	48	2 × 1	864	$495	$0.55
C	93	2 × 2	1,043	$589	$0.54
D	15	3 × 2	1,235	$739	$0.58
E	7	3 × 2	1,500	$810	$0.53
A*	36	1 × 1	744	$495	$0.63
B*	8	2 × 1	864	$549	$0.61
C*	15	2 × 2	1,043	$639	$0.59
D*	1	3 × 2	1,235	$789	$0.64
E*	1	3 × 2	1,500	$875	$0.58
	356		317,780	$184,853	$0.58

According to the unit rent roll above, the property could collect $184,853 per month if it were to collect all the rents at market. In looking at the actual potential rental income for the property, however, we found out that the property, if it was collected at 100 percent, could only make $169,085 per month. That was a difference of $15,768 per month, and $189,216 per year!

What the seller did, and this is common, was raise the rents in their system to reflect higher market rents. But they were not leasing at those rents. This created what was commonly referred to as a loss to lease. A loss to lease is the difference between what could theoretically be collected at 100 percent of market rents and what could actually be collected based on the real rents listed on the physical leases.

Many people who are buying their first multifamily acquisition do not catch subtle details like this. It's not that the brokers were lying. Those were the market rents, but the property was a long way from realizing those rents and it would take at least two years of good rent growth to realize them because we couldn't raise the rents until either someone moved out or needed to renew their lease.

Could you imagine if we hadn't noticed the difference between market rents and the potential rental income on the property? We would've collected $189,216 less than our expectations every year if we had relied on the seller pro forma. That would have been $189,216 less per year in income than we had expected. Based on a 6 percent capitalization rate, that would have meant we would have overpaid by *$3 million*! It might have been the difference between being able to pay the mortgage in the first year and not being able to—now that's a scary proposition.

All of this is to say that when you are making your offer obtain all the actual financial documentation for the property operations that you can. Don't rely on what is initially supplied to you by the seller. Doing so could blow your deal out of the water once reality sets in and could literally cost you millions of dollars. As it was, we were able to use this and some other items we discovered in the due diligence process to negotiate a significant reduction in the purchase price.

Again take a look at my first book. It will give you a detailed account of all the things to look for when analyzing a property's financials. In the book, I spell out my 5-Step Property Evaluation Process:

- Verify the property's income
- Verify the property's expenses
- Determine net operating income
- Use the capitalization rate to find the value
- Calculate the loan payment and your rate of return

Once we had completed our 5-Step Property Evaluation, we communicated our offer for the property in a non-binding letter of intent. For me, such a letter of intent is preferable to rushing straight into a purchase and sale agreement. In a letter of intent you map out the deal points in an easy-to-read format. Generally, this can be done without an attorney or at the most with a quick review by your attorney. This will save you a lot of money if your offer is not accepted. Even better, when it comes time to draft a purchase and sale agreement and your attorney is on the clock, the major points of the deal are already established. This makes the process much smoother and less expensive when it comes to legal fees.

The non-binding letter of intent is meant to be a document that engages the seller in conversation. It is not the final offer on your part, nor will the seller generally accept your first offer. The offer in the letter is meant to be open to negotiation. Generally it will detail at a high level the basic deal points such as offer price, due diligence time frame, escrow deposit amount, and any contingencies time frames you might have. (Later in this chapter I'll get more into due diligence and contingencies). The sooner you can get a letter of intent into a seller's hands the better. I usually fax or have the letter hand-delivered. The negotiation will take some time—in fact, don't be surprised if it takes weeks, so the sooner you can start the better. Time is money after all. You can view sample letters of intent on my Web site, kenmcelroy.com.

Keep in mind that the letter of intent is generally not binding on either you or the seller. That means that if the seller gets a better offer, or doesn't like your offer, they don't have to give you the time of day. This actually happened on our Oklahoma City acquisition. We spent weeks negotiating with the seller. He didn't like the fact that we didn't want to pay his asking price. He was convinced he could find a buyer who would be willing to pay full price. We were unwilling to do so and walked from the deal. When you have numbers behind you, this isn't hard to do. Emotions cause you to make stupid decisions. Not facts. A couple of months later the seller contacted us again offering to sell the property to us at our original offer. He couldn't find a buyer. We were happy to oblige him.

It is much better to take your time and make sure that you are comfortable with the deal through the letter of intent. Since purchase and sale agreements are binding and are generally accompanied with an escrow deposit on your part, you should be absolutely sure you are ready to move forward with the deal. There are plenty of properties to purchase, but you probably don't have a lot of $200,000 deposits to lose if you decide to back out of a purchase and sale agreement.

The Purchase and Sale Agreement (PSA)

The purchase and sale agreement is the most important document you will draft in the process of acquiring a multifamily property. Of course, *you* won't be drafting it. Your attorney will. The PSA will be the culmination of your letter of intent negotiations. All the deal specifics will be hammered out during the drafting period of the PSA. It will clearly list and explain what is expected of both the buyer and seller. It is a substantial document that will be many pages long.

The PSA will explain how the seller will provide information to you about the property such as financials, engineer's reports, and other pertinent documents. Most importantly, it will create a timeline of critical dates that includes the date your deposit becomes nonrefundable, when the due diligence period starts and ends, and the date you are required to close escrow. While the negotiations may not take as long as the letter of intent negotiations do, they will be just as important and just as intense. You do not want to do this alone. A small investment in the services of an attorney will save you a lot of money down the road.

Here is a list of the items that should be included in the purchase and sale agreement:

- Purchase price
- Down payment
- Amount of the initial escrow deposit
- Title company information
- Agreed-upon time frames and dates for when the deposit goes non-refundable, the due diligence period and waiving of contingencies (explained on the next page), and close of escrow
- The way in which rents, taxes, insurance, and security deposits will be prorated—these should be split between the buyer and seller

- Whether the loan is being assumed or if it's new financing
- Contents of the title report and when it will be delivered
- Definition of the financing contingencies
- Time frame on when all documents required for due diligence will be delivered, including all books and records, rental agreements, operating statements, rent rolls, personal property inventories, service contracts, utility contracts, ALTA (boundary) survey, environmental reports, architectural plans, and engineering reports and appraisals
- Time frames for physical inspections—both interior and exterior
- Information on lead paint, mold, radon, or other allergens

As you can see, the list is pretty substantial and something you don't want to navigate alone. Your attorney and broker will be helpful during this time in clarifying language that might be confusing and watching your back to make sure you aren't getting taken for a ride.

Take special care to consult your attorney on contingencies. Contingencies are provisions within a contract that give you the ability to cancel a deal in the event of unforeseen circumstances. This could be something as simple as not being able to obtain financing for the deal to the presence of serious environmental issues. The first example is referred to as a loan contingency, and the second is referred to as a due diligence contingency. Contingencies are absolutely critical and it is a very bad idea not to have them. I've known many people who failed to work contingencies into their contract and when they ran into a deal-killer, they lost their deposits. That could mean losing hundreds of thousands of dollars, all because you didn't structure the PSA the right way.

Once you have successfully negotiated the purchase and sale agreement, you will be ready to execute the agreement and place the property in escrow. This will require a deposit on your part, generally in the hundreds of thousands of dollars. But this money is fully refundable if you have structured the PSA well and with the consultation of your attorney. With the right structure, a PSA will allow you plenty of time and room to back out of a deal if you have just cause. With the property in escrow, you are now ready to begin the real work. Your due diligence period begins.

Due Diligence—Do or Die

As I mentioned earlier, due diligence is one of the most essential parts of the purchase process. This is your one shot to find out every little detail there is to know about the property, and it's the process that will ultimately lead to your decision to move forward with the acquisition or to move on to the next deal. In this section I will take you through the due diligence checklist I use on every property I acquire. I will teach you how to evaluate a property and, as the song says, "know when to hold 'em, know when to fold 'em."

During the due diligence period, there are two aspects of any property that you will dig into—the operations and the physical property. Both are vitally important. Performing due diligence of the operations requires you to thoroughly review every aspect of the property's books and records. You want to verify everything that you based your original purchase offer on. Additionally, you will be using the information gathered during this process to start formulating your operating budget by categorizing the property's income and expenses.

Physical due diligence requires you to inspect every nook and cranny. That means you will need to walk every square inch of the property and physically observe the exterior and interior of the buildings. You will also need to have professionals take a look at things like the roofs, pavement, plumbing, and so on. You will be looking for anything that might have to be repaired or replaced once you take over the property. If major items present themselves, you will be able to use them as bargaining tools to lower your initial purchase offer or to have them fixed before the close of escrow.

You might be thinking this is a process that could take months. You're right. There are numerous things that need to be accomplished during the vital due diligence time. The problem is you don't have months. Generally, you have a thirty-day window to find out all the things you need before you are required to waive your contingencies and your deposit goes nonrefundable. It would be impossible to accomplish by yourself. Thankfully, you have a team you can utilize.

In my company we have a team that is dedicated specifically to the due diligence process. They perform the due diligence on every property that we go to contract on. This team includes people from my property management company, my lawyers, members of my construction team, and my finance experts. I couldn't accomplish the work needed in such a short time without them. While in my case I have my own employees to perform this work, there are also property management companies that can do it for a fee.

Utilize the property manager on your team to assist you with this process. A little up-front investment of money in this area will save you money down the line. Through our due diligence process on our Oklahoma City property, we discovered almost $800,000 in deferred maintenance that either had to be fixed by the owner or reduced from the purchase price. That relatively small due diligence investment of $20,000 saved us $800,000!

The List

On each and every property that I perform due diligence on, I have a list of all the items that need to be addressed. Having a list is vital to the process. There are far too many details and variables to be able to keep them all in my head, or even on a piece of yellow legal paper. I'm going to run you through my personal due diligence list and go into detail about the things you should be looking for and why. This is the very same list that we used when performing the due diligence on our recent acquisition in Oklahoma City, the very same list that helped us to find $800,000 in deferred maintenance. It's a very important list!

LEASING INFORMATION AND POLICIES

This can be done in two phases. One from the comfort of your own home or office, the other needs to be completed on-site. In phase one you receive and review all the information on the leasing policies of the property, the actual lease itself and any other paperwork, the current rent rolls, security deposit ledger, each resident ledger showing the history of rent payment, and the current rents and concessions. In phase two, you physically audit the files on-site and compare them to the information supplied to you in the reports. You review the actual application of each resident, the credit and criminal background check, the individual leases and addenda, and match the information to your ledgers.

Once you receive all of the leases and the reports on the property rents, you will want to make sure to compare them to the financials that were supplied to you since you based your initial offer on them. You are attempting to verify the income of the property. Make sure that the rents total up to what the financials have listed. You will want to begin compiling a spreadsheet encompassing all the units in the property. This will be your "one-stop shop" once you begin your file audit. Compile all the information you receive into this spreadsheet. List the rent, concessions (if any), deposits, pet rents, and other types of discounts like preferred employer or employee discounts. This will be a valuable tool for you down the road.

When you have a completed unit-by-unit spreadsheet listing all the information, you're ready to begin your file audit. The file audit is extremely important because you are comparing the physical contracts that are binding on you and the resident, not the rent roll that you were provided. You would be surprised how many property managers are absolutely horrendous at keeping files. I can't tell you how many times I've run into situations where leases aren't signed, rents are listed differently than what is in the computer or on the rent roll, and background checks were not performed, or were ignored. The list goes on and on.

When you do your file audit you will meticulously go through each physical file that is on-site. Make sure to bring a laptop and add another set of columns to your spreadsheet so as to compare what was provided to you by the seller and what is actually in the files themselves. As I mentioned, don't be surprised if there are plenty of discrepancies. Oftentimes there are explanations, but then again, oftentimes there are not. There are plenty of managers out there who are simply negligent. I've done file audits where certain files were missing completely. They were nowhere to be found on the entire property. That meant there was no way to know if the residents in the unit were approved, if they had a criminal background, if they were supposed to be there at all, or even if the unit was vacant.

When you are doing the file audit you will also want to verify the following:

- Your physical lease rents match the rent roll provided. Your net operating income depends on it.
- A background, credit, and sex offender check on every resident has been performed and placed on file. Failure to do this could affect your future occupancy.

- Deposits match—you inherit this liability from the seller.
- Who is actually living in the unit and if they are on the lease.
- If there are any notices such as for eviction or breach of policy.
- Do the residents have a pet addendum? What kind of pet and what size?

These things will help you to formulate an idea of the type of people that make up the resident profile of the property. They will also help you to red-flag certain units that you will want to keep an eye on if and when you take over ownership.

Once your file audit is complete and all the information obtained from the files is analyzed, you will want to compare the information provided by the seller with the physical information that you obtained. Note any discrepancies and send a list of them to the seller for explanation. These can be as simple as a $1,000 difference in actual security deposits collected and what is referenced on the lease, or as major as significant differences between the provided rents and the actual rents listed on the leases.

While doing our file audit for the Oklahoma City property we discovered that there was a discrepancy regarding the rents listed on the rent rolls and the actual leases in over 10 percent of the units, forty in total. Some of these were minor differences of $10 per month; others were major differences in excess of $100 per month. When all was said and done, we discovered that the rent rolls initially supplied to us reflected rents significantly higher than what was actually on the leases. Since the physical leases are what are legally binding, not what was stated on the rent roll, the difference for us was a negative swing in our projected annual rental income—and a significant difference in the value.

I don't want to suggest that the seller was intentionally fudging the rent rolls. I know the seller and he is a stand-up businessman. There are a number of explanations for discrepancies. In some cases, it is a clerical error when entering the leasing information into a computer. In others, it can be that the income is allocated to another category so that the net result is the same. Whatever the case may be, the fact remains that the discrepancies existed, and that they represented a major change in the value of the property. If we had not performed a file audit we would have been over $33,000 off our investment projections in the first year.

FINANCIAL AND OPERATING REPORTS

When performing your due diligence there are a number of financial and operating reports that you will want to obtain in order to get a clear picture of how the property has operated over the years. These will enable you to increase your understanding of trends in the market and the property itself. What you will collect will depend on the property that you are acquiring.

Here is a list of the items that I generally require from the seller:

- At least three years of actual annual financial statements
- Certified rent rolls
- The most recent balance sheet
- The year-to-date general ledger
- Current year budget
- Delinquency report
- Prepaid rent report
- Month-to-date collections report
- Current vacancy report
- Security deposit report
- Twelve-month potential renter traffic report
- Bank statements and reconciliations for the last twelve months
- All loan documentation
- A signed affidavit attesting that all the above are accurate

You will want to use these reports in order to verify the information that was initially provided to you by the seller. Additionally, these reports will be a valuable resource as you are preparing your financial forecast for the property and determining the operating budget you will use once you own the property.

Make sure to note the last item on the list. This is for your protection. As I discussed earlier, there is no way for you to actually know if the data given to you is accurate. There is a lot at stake here. If the data is falsified then you could really be hurt once you take over the property. There are plenty of horror stories about financials that were falsified by hundreds of thousands of dollars in order to get a higher purchase price. The results can be disastrous for the buyer once they own the property. A difference of $100,000 per year can be the difference between paying your mortgage or not.

If you are not fully versed in the process of reading financials, then, by all means, utilize those on your investment team who are. Your accountant and property manager team members will be a help in this area. Also, in the meantime, you should learn yourself. Have them go over the information with you. Being able to read a financial is a key to success in business and in multifamily investment. Without that skill you are at a significant disadvantage.

INCOME AND EXPENSE ITEMS

On any multifamily property there will be miscellaneous items that will provide "other income" such as profit-sharing contracts with phone and cable companies, washer and dryer income, pet rent, and utility income. It will be in your best interest to obtain these contracts and verify that they match what the financial statements provided by the seller are indicating. Additionally, you will want to see what the terms of the agreements are and whether they are transferable at sale. You need to take into account lost revenue streams from contracts that do not transfer at sale and find out what the new terms may be, and how they will affect your income. In many cases these agreements can be five to ten years in length and have automatic renewal clauses. Also, the seller may have even received an up-front incentive just for signing the agreement. The balance of such incentives should be prorated to you at close of escrow.

Conversely, you need to do the same thing with the expenses of the property. In the grand scheme of things, verifying the expenses that the property has is much more important than the miscellaneous income. Income can be manipulated. Expenses, however, are generally static. That means that there is not a whole lot you can do to change them. Here is a list of all items related to expenses that I verify when I am purchasing a property:

- Utility bills for the last three years with account numbers
- Staff names, positions, salaries, and benefits
- Three-year history of capital improvements, and list of items replaced in the last three years (refrigerators, carpets, and so forth)
- List of any and all advertising and marketing contracts
- Management agreement for the property
- Property tax information

- Insurance information and premium amount, as well as information on any past losses
- Three-year work order history
- List of recurring maintenance issues
- List of required homeowners association memberships and dues
- List of personal property to be transferred
- Office equipment leases (copiers, computers, and so on)
- List of supplies purchased in the last twelve months

Once you have received this information you will want to keep it on file, compile it, and compare it to the financials the seller provided. You want to be sure that when you take over ownership there are no expenses that are unaccounted for that will throw your financial forecast out of whack. Again, sometimes discrepancies can be large. Other times they can be small.

For instance, on our Oklahoma City property the expenses were reflected accurately. When we received the personal property inventories, however, we noticed many washer and dryers in several units were missing from the list. We inquired as to why. It ended up being a simple oversight, but since the inventory list becomes part of the binding purchase and sale agreement, we wanted to be sure they were included. Purchasing new washers and dryers would have been a small expense, but why pay for something if you don't have to. It always pays to be diligent—I guess that's why they call it due diligence.

STUDIES

Any multifamily property that you are thinking of acquiring will likely have a number of pertinent studies required. These are usually property condition reports, Phase I (environmental), zoning reports, title reports, ALTA surveys, appraisals, and so forth. In these reports you will be looking for issues that may cost you after you close or issues that could affect your ability to obtain financing, like the presence of hazardous materials or toxins. Additionally, if they are available you will want to receive reports on the soil composition and the structural integrity of the buildings themselves. These should always be compiled by third-party inspectors and engineers. The presence of these types of materials could be a deal-killer. The last thing you want to deal with is remediating potentially harmful units. Just the threat of lawsuits alone should send you running for the hills.

I've backed out of deals because of information that I found in studies like these. In one instance, we found out a property we were purchasing in Arizona was built on what is commonly referred to as "expansive soil." Basically that's a complicated way of saying that the soil expands and contracts more than normal and can cause substantial foundation problems. You don't want a house built on sand! Because we knew this, we paid special attention to the foundations when doing our physical inspections. We found hairline cracks throughout the property that were an indication of a much bigger and very expensive problem. We walked away from the deal, thankful that we had caught the problem before it was too late.

LEGAL AND CONSTRUCTION DOCUMENTATION

Prior to the close of escrow—COE—there are a number of documents that you will want to obtain so that you will have them on hand when you take ownership. These include:

- The legal description—this will be in the purchase and sale agreement as well
- Title report
- Seller's certificate verifying that the property meets all state and local codes
- Copies of any zoning letters
- Copies of all utility letters
- Any pending litigation
- Certificates of occupancy
- Site plans
- Copy of original building plans, if any
- Copies of all warranties, if any

Once again, it's important to gather these documents in case of any legal disputes and one of them may be required to aid your defense.

If a property you are purchasing is newly constructed, there are a number of additional construction-related documents that you will want to collect. You will want copies of the following:

- Change orders (overruns in construction expenses)
- Construction manager's report
- Building/developer permits
- General contractor's contract
- Soil and structural tests
- Permits
- Mechanical, plumbing, electrical approvals
- Fire inspections
- City approvals
- Truss calculations (support beams)
- Safety data sheet for materials used in construction
- Operating manuals
- Service contracts and agreements (landscaping, pest control, and so on)
- Warranties

Once you have obtained all the items on your due diligence list, reviewed and analyzed them, and incorporated them into your operation projections, you will still have to complete your physical inspection of both the exterior and interior of the buildings. This is the time to look for "the good, the bad, and the ugly." Leave no stone unturned. Walk *every* unit and observe *every* aspect of the property's exterior. I can't stress how important this is. Remember, if my partner and I hadn't performed the physical inspections of the Oklahoma City property, we would never have discovered the $800,000 in deferred maintenance until it was too late. We would've had no one to blame but ourselves.

EXTERIOR INSPECTIONS

Chances are you aren't an expert on examining the exterior condition of a building. I know I'm not. Unless the roof is completely caved in, it will probably look pretty good to me. When you are doing your exterior inspections you should be engaging the expertise of people who specialize in installing, maintaining, and repairing every aspect of a property. You should create a list of categories that will need inspecting and organize meetings with subcontractors to inspect the property and obtain bids for any work that will need to be completed. The best part is that obtaining bids is typically free. It's considered a normal process for earning your business. Here is a list of general categories you will want to inspect:

- Plumbing
- Electrical
- Roofs
- Paint and siding
- Landscaping
- Asphalt and concrete work
- Heating and air-conditioning units
- Pest problems
- Fire protection systems

When you are obtaining bids for these items, don't just rely on one company. Take the time and effort to meet with a number of companies and obtain competing bids. This will save you money. At the very least, you can use one company's bid to negotiate a lower fee with another company. This can be overwhelming, so this is another opportunity to use your team!

If there are any major items on the property that need addressing, now is the time to find out. Not after you own the property. In the case of our Oklahoma City property we found a number of exterior items that would either need to be completed or that we wanted to see completed. The property had some major repairs that were needed to the landscaping, roofs, parking areas, pools, and sport court facility. Just the necessary repairs to the exterior aspects of the property were $282,834. You might be laughing to yourself about how specific that dollar amount is, but we weren't. We obtained that amount by having experts on-site to give us bids. In turn we were able to use those bids to negotiate a reduction in the purchase price and to have some of the work covered after closing by an escrow account in the seller's name. If I hadn't taken the time to contract professionals to do the inspection work, I probably never would have caught it.

INTERIOR INSPECTIONS

I've said it before and I'll say it again: You need to walk every unit on the property. Period. You will be amazed at the incredibly weird things that are hiding behind apartment doors. I've been doing this for over twenty-five years and just when I think I've seen it all, something else pops up. I've been in units where there was so much trash you couldn't see the floor. I've seen reptiles roaming freely, and holes punched through the wall of one unit into the other. I've been in apartments that were completely gutted and had evidence of heavy drug use. You name it and I've seen it.

When we are purchasing a property we walk every unit and make general notes of their condition. I've found that the most efficient way to do this is to use a unit inspection form I call the "Vacant Unit Condition Report".

Once you have finished your interior inspections, you should take all the unit inspection forms and compile the data you've collected into a spreadsheet. We prefer to use something like the form on the next page to indicate the condition of each aspect of a unit's interior. That way we are able to simply mark the column that applies and tally up the numbers at the end. It makes it much easier to estimate the dollar amount that will be needed to fix any interior issues.

Just like with the exterior of our Oklahoma City property, we found many issues that needed addressing in the interiors. One major issue was that the sub-flooring on all the second-floor levels needed replacement because the Gyp-Crete, a lightweight concrete substance, was cracking. This is a major-ticket item. The flooring expert on our team estimated the replacement cost would be $1,000 per unit, or $150,000 for just that one item. Additionally, there were a number of isolated items that needed to be replaced such as cabinets, sinks, carpets, appliances, drywall, and countertops. All of these added up. As I've said earlier, our exterior and interior inspections resulted in us finding close to $800,000 in deferred maintenance that we would have otherwise been responsible for. It could have been a huge disaster. Thankfully we did our due diligence. These would have been costs we would have incurred as each resident moved out.

I hope that this chapter has impressed upon you the importance of the due diligence process. If you were to take nothing else away from this book, the concepts in this chapter would be worth the read. Due diligence that is done properly will save you millions of dollars.

	Vacant Unit Condition Report			Circle				
Property Name	_____				Vacant	Yes	No	
Unit Number	_____				Rent Ready	Yes	No	
					Pet(s)		_____	

	Condition Rating			
Item	**Check One**			**Comments**
KITCHEN	Replace	Poor	Good	
Floors				
Paint/Walls/Ceiling				
Cabinets				
Stove/Oven				
Microwave				
Refrigerator				
Dishwasher				
Lights				
Countertop				
Plumbing (disposal/faucet/leaks)				
Doors/Windows/Screens				
Other				
LIVING/DINING AND HALL	Replace	Poor	Good	**Comments**
Doors/Windows/Screens				
Fireplace				
Paint/Walls/Ceiling				
Floors				
Other				
BATHROOM 1	Replace	Poor	Good	**Comments**
Floors				
Paint/Walls/Ceiling				
Sink & Vanity				
Tub & Shower				
Lights				
Toilet				
Cabinets				
Doors/Windows/Screens				
Other				
BATHROOM 2	Replace	Poor	Good	**Comments**
Floors				
Paint/Walls/Ceiling				
Sink & Vanity				
Tub & Shower				
Lights				
Toilet				
Cabinets				
Doors/Windows/Screens				
Other				
BEDROOM 1	Replace	Poor	Good	**Comments**
Lights				
Doors/Windows/Screens				
Closet Doors				
Floor				
Paint/Walls/Ceiling				
Drapes				
Paint/Walls				
Other				
BEDROOM 2	Replace	Poor	Good	**Comments**
Lights				
Doors/Windows/Screens				
Closet Doors				
Floor				
Paint/Walls/Ceiling				
Drapes				
Paint/Walls				
Other				
OTHER	Replace	Poor	Good	**Comments**
Hot Water Heater				
HVAC				
Patio/Balcony/Storage				
Washer/Dryer Hook Up				
Washer/Dryer Included				

As an illustration, here is a chart that sums up the money we saved by performing our due diligence on the Oklahoma City property:

Annual difference between market rents and actual rents	$ 189,216
Exterior deferred maintenance	$ 282,834
Interior deferred maintenance	$ 503,312
Total	$ 975,362

We were able to recapture all of these potential costs to us through renegotiations with the seller on the purchase price. As I mentioned, at first he didn't like it and walked from the deal. But we had the facts behind us so we weren't disappointed. We were relieved. We had moved on to looking at other opportunities when the seller came to us a few months later and told us he was willing to accept our offer after all. Nothing is more satisfying than a job well done. The thing about this process is that the next buyer, if thorough, would find these items as well. In the end, the seller could go through multiple buyers and deal with the same long process.

Chapter 8

Equity and Financing

At the same time you are performing your due diligence you will be actively engaging lenders and potential investors in order to raise the money necessary to purchase your property. Generally you will have a loan that ranges from 70 to 80 percent of the sales price, so if you are going to purchase the property you will need to raise 20 percent or more in investor equity for the down payment and capital reserves, which we'll get into later, or pony up the money yourself.

If you're anything like I was before I purchased my first apartment building you're probably scoffing at the prospect of being able to make a multimillion-dollar investment. Well, I have good news for you. As the old saying goes, there's more than one way to skin a cat. In large multifamily investing there are a couple things that are in your favor.

First off, loans on investments like multifamily properties aren't entirely based on your credit. They are based on the asset itself. That means you don't have to be a millionaire. You just have to find a property that will make you one! If you have a solid property and an excellent business plan, you will be able to find a loan. Secondly, money adds up quickly. If you have a solid business plan there will be investors that will want to be a part of the acquisition.

If you have a network of people who are looking for solid investment opportunities, you will have no problem raising money for your acquisition.

Don't have a network of people who are looking to invest? Well then you're out of luck. Close the book . . . just kidding. There is a great option available to you, one that will enable you both to invest in large multifamily investments and start to develop a network of investors. You can invest in a limited liability company (LLC), a single-purpose entity that can be formed to purchase a multifamily investment. In many cases you can participate in such a joint venture or syndication with as little as $25,000—that's basically a down payment on a house.

If you go into such an investment, make sure the promoter, the person putting the deal together, offers you a private placement memorandum. This is the required legal document for offering syndications and joint ventures in real estate. If they can't offer you such a document, stay away; they are amateurs you don't want to place your money with. But if done properly, with the right documentation, these types of investments can work out well for everyone involved.

Sound too good to be true? Well it's not. That's exactly how we rounded up our equity for the Oklahoma City property. We formed an LLC—as we do for every property we acquire—and asked our equity members to invest in the new LLC. For the Oklahoma City property we have a total of twenty investors. Some of them have only $25,000 invested. Others have over $1 million. What they now all have in common is that they own a portion of a 356-unit apartment building in Oklahoma City valued at over $13 million. I welcome you to visit my Web site, kenmcelroy.com, and look at this property.

Whether you are planning on being part of the equity position in an LLC, or planning to form one and raise equity for your own acquisition, here are the basics of how it works. (I should note here that this is just a general overview—please consult your attorney on the specifics of setting up a limited liability company. It sounds simple, but it's not.)

When we formed our LLC for the Oklahoma City property we consulted our attorney. He was able to get all the paperwork in order to form the entity. He was also essential in the drafting of the operating agreement. The operating agreement is a vital document in a transaction like this. It spells out who has the right to manage the operations of the LLC, defines the purpose and operations of the company, and lays out the structure for the distribution of profits, among other things.

The way we structure our deals is to find the property and get it into escrow with our own funds. If you do not have the money required for escrow, then find a business partner who does. Once we have the property secured, we begin soliciting our investors. In the case of the Oklahoma City property we had all the equity we needed in literally one day. We earned this, however, over many years of relationship building and a proven track record. Your first deal will take some selling and work, but if you have a solid deal you'll be able to find investors.

My team helps me develop an investor summary, which is also our business plan that explains every aspect of the property acquisition. We send interested investors a confidentiality agreement if they want to view this—even Robert and Kim Kiyosaki have to sign one for each deal. The lesson here is to never give away your hand for free. We work hard to find the right deal and don't want someone to use our offering for their own solicitation. It is meant for their eyes only. Our confidentiality agreement also includes an accredited investor qualification form. We wish everyone could invest with us, but we have seen too many people stretch themselves too far because they were not in a financial position to invest. It is our policy that you have to be financially fit to invest the relatively large sums required to buy into an LLC. You don't have to be rich, but you do have to be stable.

Once we receive the confidentiality agreements we send out the investor summary/business plan for review. (For information on how to prepare one of these plans on your own, see Garrett Sutton's *The ABC's of Writing Winning Business Plans*.) This is an exhilarating time. Our potential investors will be calling us to discuss the particulars of the deal. With their questions answered, the potential investors determine whether the deal is right for them or not. If they wish to invest we send out what is referred to as a "subscription agreement" that will give us their information for their entity, and their equity commitment. This is usually sent back to us by the investor with wiring instructions for a deposit that is placed in a trust account specifically for that property.

As I've said, we usually have investors that are chomping at the bit to be a part of these opportunities. In the case of the Oklahoma City opportunity, it was subscribed overnight. The reason investors signed on so fast was that the projected returns were so great and the business plan was thorough.

If you are forming an LLC in order to raise equity for your own acquisition, then you will need to be working toward obtaining financing at the same time. So far we've reviewed the necessary steps to purchase a property, including the letter of intent and the purchase and sale agreement, and the importance of the due diligence process. Now let's look at the financing process.

Financing

Financing a multifamily property is not simple. You will need the help of your mortgage broker. When we are purchasing a building we always turn to our mortgage broker. They will be able to obtain multiple quotes for you to review and help you find the best financing available for your business plan. When you are purchasing a property there is one of two ways that you will obtain financing:

1. Obtaining a new loan or loans
2. Assuming the existing loan

OBTAINING A NEW LOAN

Many times, terms of the existing loan will not be favorable on a property. You will have to seek out new financing to purchase the property. That's what it means when a selling broker's marketing piece says, "Available for purchase on an all-cash basis." You don't literally need to have the cash sitting in your bank account. You do, however, need to be able to provide the funds for purchase through private equity and a new loan.

As we've already talked about raising the equity for the down payment, we won't get into that here. While you're soliciting funds for the down payment you will also be working toward shoring up your financing for the project. Ultimately, the difference between your loan and the purchase price will determine your equity needed. That means you will have to contact your mortgage broker and have him or her begin to shop for loans. You'll have a good idea of what kind of financing you're looking for since you should have already analyzed the property's financials and developed a business plan. Communicate your needs to your mortgage broker and he or she will do their best to find a loan that matches your needs. This is the time to fully disclose any and all issues (personal and property related) to your mortgage broker.

Once your mortgage broker has obtained loan quotes you will need to review them and determine which loan you want to pursue. Once you have picked the loan, the lender will provide you with a document called a loan term sheet. This will be issued early on in your due diligence process, and it is one of the most important documents you will review. It will have the following items detailed:

- Requested loan amount
- Minimum debt service coverage ratio
- Loan to value
- Borrower's equity amount
- Initial term/amortization and extension of initial term
- Loan constant
- Interest rate and interest rate cap/hedge
- Payments schedule
- Prepayment penalty
- Guarantor
- Borrower reporting requirements
- Immediate repair reserve and replacement reserves
- Tax/Insurance reserves
- Evidence of insurance clause
- Management agreement requirement
- Third-party reports such as environmental, property inspection, and appraisals
- Origination fee
- Deposits required
- Committee approvals
- Any additional conditions such as a business plan, performance criteria, and so forth

You're probably wondering why I just listed a page's worth of "lender lingo." I did it because that's what you'll see when you get your term sheet. It's complicated, and if you don't understand portions of the list on page 125, you won't understand your loan fully. That's a scary proposition. Use your attorney to review the loan term sheet. He or she will be able to tell you the legal implications of the various clauses. Additionally, your mortgage broker will be an invaluable asset in explaining the document in plain English. For a sample version of a loan term sheet, visit my Web site, kenmcelroy.com.

It should be noted here that just because you have a term sheet, it doesn't mean you have a loan. Your lender will want to review the property and determine whether it wants to move forward with funding the project. The lender will have many items that it will require you to provide for them for review. They'll have their own consultants for the property condition report, and have their own environmental hygienists, engineers, appraisers, and underwriter go to the property and inspect it. They'll also ask you to provide financial statements, rent rolls, payroll schedules, your business plan, and other items regarding the operations of the property. In essence, they will be doing their own due diligence of the property. They want to know what they are getting into before they give you a final loan commitment letter.

Once the lender has satisfied all their conditions on funding the property they will issue you a loan commitment letter. Make sure to work a contingency into your purchase and sale agreement that states you can walk away from the deal and retain your earnest money if you're unable to acquire financing. You wouldn't want to lose your deposit money because you couldn't obtain a loan. This happens more often than you might think. I don't want to say you're at the mercy of the lender—but you are—in many respects.

ASSUMING A LOAN

It's not uncommon to find a property that has an assumable loan. That means you'll assume the existing financing on the property after close of escrow. There are many reasons this might be to your advantage. The biggest is that you have the opportunity to obtain a lower interest rate than what the market is offering. Additionally, you'll be able to review the loan documents during the due diligence process.

We assumed the loan on our Oklahoma City property. The interest rate was a full percentage point lower than anything we could have obtained in the current market. When you are talking about multimillion-dollar loans, that's a tremendous amount of savings. Something you have to be leery of, however, is when assuming a loan, there may be an assumption fee. Make sure to have the mortgage broker on your team analyze whether it is more beneficial for you to assume the loan and pay the penalty, or to get new financing completely.

Additionally, when you assume an existing loan, you may be facing a large gap between the purchase price and the loan amount. In these cases you will either have to raise more equity than the standard 20 percent of the purchase price, or you will have to try to obtain a secondary mortgage—if possible. Not all financial institutions will provide secondary financing on loan assumptions. Can you begin to see why your mortgage broker is so valuable?

Whether you are obtaining new financing, or assuming an existing loan, financing is a vital part of your investment and ultimately will determine your down payment. The loan you obtain will often make or break a deal. Be diligent and consult your experts. They will be able to steer you away from potential disasters when it comes to financing your investment.

Close of Escrow (COE)

Once you have developed your investment summary/business plan, obtained a loan, and rounded up your equity, it will be time to close escrow on the property. This is the big day. After close of escrow, COE, the property will be yours, along with all the advantages (and all the problems). Closing escrow on a large property is a complicated process. At a minimum, set aside a whole day. There are a couple of things that will make the process a little smoother.

Obtain a copy of the Department of Housing and Urban Development (HUD) statement at least a day before the close of escrow. HUD requires title companies to produce a HUD statement (which essentially is a closing statement) for each buyer that shows all the costs and credits associated with the closing. This will include things like title insurance fees, appraisals, processing fees, prorations, and a month or two of your mortgage payment. On a large multifamily deal there are other items that you will want to pay particular attention to as well:

Rent Prorations	If you are closing on the middle of the month you will have worked out a proration schedule for the rents that have been collected for the month. Since rents for the entire month are generally collected at the beginning of the month, if you close on the 15th, you will need a credit at closing for half the total collected rental income. The seller may also want to work out a deal to get a prorated portion of any delinquent rents.
Security Deposits	All of the security deposits that were collected by the prior owner need to come to you at close of escrow (COE) because you will now be responsible for either giving them back when someone moves out or using them toward damages in a vacated unit.
Taxes	Varies by state—be aware of the proration.
Insurance	Typically paid a full year in advance at close of escrow and then through a monthly impound.
Capital Expenses	If your business plan calls for capital improvements, the bank will require a detailed record of those improvements and a cost estimate. The funds will be placed in an escrow account and released to you by the bank in phases. Make sure the HUD statement reflects the contract amount.
Deferred Maintenance (if any)	Same as Capital Expenses.
Brokerage Commissions	The purchase and sale agreement will stipulate the amounts brokers will receive as commissions. Double-check that the amounts on the HUD statement are correct.

When you are reviewing the HUD statement, make sure the amounts on it reflect what has been agreed upon between you and the seller. If there are any changes that need to be made, make sure to contact the title company and the seller without delay. You want there to be as little possible to change on the day of closing. Also, make sure to have your accountant and your attorney review the statement. The more eyes the better.

Here is a short timeline for the day of closing:

- Sign the closing documents
- Review the HUD statement
- Wire your money

The last thing you want to happen on the day of closing is for something to go wrong and to have to deal with any glitches in getting your funds to the table. Make sure to close the loop. Contact the title agency and *confirm that the wire has been received into the escrow account*.

Even with all the preparation you've done prior to the close of escrow, there will generally be something that needs to be discussed on the final HUD statement. Make sure to have copies of your estimated HUD statement with you so that you can discuss any discrepancies. Sometimes there will be extra costs associated with the closing that you did not anticipate. Other times you will need less or even more money than expected. Just be sure to be diligent and verify that all amounts are correct.

Make sure to have your lawyer available so that you can run any questions on the closing documents by him or her. Here are the documents that you will want to review with your lawyer at the closing table. You will want to review all of these as applicable before you wire your money to the title company:

- Special warranty deed
- Affidavit of property value
- Tenants in common agreement (TIC) if applicable (this is another type of ownership)
- Memorandum of TIC agreement if applicable
- Loan agreement
- Promissory note

- Guaranty agreement
- Environmental indemnity agreement
- Deed of trust
- Assignment management
- Borrower's certification
- Contribution
- Closing escrow agreement
- Uniform Commercial Code (UCC) statement
- Settlement statement (HUD)

Once you have signed the papers, the property is effectively yours. All that will be left is for the lender to fund your loan and the title to be recorded. Congratulations: You are now a multifamily investor! Now what?

The purpose of this book is not to get into the specifics of operating an apartment building. I touch on the subject of property management in my earlier book, *The ABC's of Real Estate Investing*, and I'm in the process of writing a book that covers the topic in detail. In addition to the market, the way a property is managed can be the determining factor as to whether it will grow in value or not. If you are not a professional property manager, then you need to hire one. Hopefully you have not waited till the day of closing to figure this out like that investor who purchased a property in Mesa and called me the day before closing. Your property manager is not only valuable after the close of escrow, but leading up to it as a resource for your due diligence.

By finding the right property manager to be on your team, you can take a good property and make it great just by enhancing the property's performance. Remember my example earlier in the book, the Fountains at Sun City? That property gained substantial value because we were able to manage it well. In essence we created millions in value by implementing a management plan that increased income and minimized expenses. The formula is simple; the execution is not. If you don't have the time and the experience to manage your property effectively, then don't. Doing so could mean lost value and diminished returns to you and your investors.

You might think such things are easy for me to say since I own a management company. The reason for this is that I want to have control of my investments. So I do property management full-time. I hired a local management company, however, to manage my Oklahoma City property. Since I live and work out of Phoenix, it would be unwise and inefficient for me to try and manage my one property in Oklahoma. In the end, I place good odds on the fact that I would lose more money through lost income opportunities than I pay in management fees. In this case I deferred to experts—a local, knowledgeable management company.

Chapter 9

Assembling Your Multifamily Team

If you have listened to Robert and the *Rich Dad* team at all, you know one of the essential parts of business is having a team. This certainly holds true in multifamily investing. If you try to go at this alone, you will fail. Have you ever tried to play basketball against a team all by yourself? One against five in basketball isn't very good odds—even for Michael Jordan. If you try investing in multifamily without a proper team, you run the risk of facing even worse odds.

I have a full team of professionals assembled that I consult on a daily basis. Many of them work in my company, but there are many who have their own companies or businesses as well. I would never think of purchasing a deal without consulting them. There are just too many things I could miss, and too many ways I could get taken advantage of.

In this chapter, I'll briefly cover every player that you will need on your team in order to be a successful multifamily investor. You can't assemble a team like this overnight, nor should you. Get out there, don't be shy, and make contacts with professionals who will become key players on your team. Over time you will develop business relationships that will be some of the best investments in time you've ever made.

One quick note on finding the players for your team. Don't just flip open a yellow pages and start calling companies who sound professional. That is probably the least productive way. Start asking around for referrals. You will be surprised by the wealth of knowledge that is all around you in your friends, family, and business relationships. They will be able to refer you to many of the people you will need to have an effective team. The more people you meet, the broader your network will become.

#1. Property Manager

At the end of the last chapter, I urged you to hire a property manager to professionally manage your valuable asset. The right manager will add value to your property. There is no doubt about it. But in addition to managing your property, the property manager will be useful to you in other areas as well.

Often your property manager will be well versed in the due diligence process. Utilize him or her. It will make life much easier. Property managers are, just like your broker, a wealth of information. They will know intimate details about the rental market in their area. You can obtain market surveys from them. And they will be able to keep you abreast of any changes in the rental market. Additionally, they manage properties for a living, so they will be familiar with strategies for increasing income and reducing expenses. They will be invaluable in helping you set up your operating budget and business plan.

#2. Lawyer

Finding the right lawyer is important. Your lawyer will be involved in a large part of your multifamily investments. You will use him or her to review your letter of intent, to negotiate and review purchase and sale agreements, negotiate your loan, give advice on any legal questions arising from the due diligence period, assist you with the complicated process of closing escrow, and help you set up the legal structure of your property by assisting you with operating agreements and the formation of the legal entity you will place your property in.

Not just any lawyer will do. Make sure the attorney on your team is an experienced professional practicing real estate law. The last thing you need is a lawyer who specializes in criminal defense representing you on a complicated purchase and sale agreement negotiation just because he is your brother-in-law and "could really use the business."

If none of your current contacts knows any qualified real estate attorneys, ask your broker who he or she has worked with in the past and who they might recommend. Also, you can check local multifamily trade associations. They often list members who provide legal counsel in a directory of services. Trade associations can be a valuable resource in finding members of your team.

When interviewing a lawyer it's important to ask questions that will make them a good fit for your team. Ask what kinds of deals he or she has been involved in. You will be looking for the size of the properties and the number of deals. Where he or she got their degree is really not that important. What's important is experience. The last thing you want is a novice.

#3. Accountant

Unless you want to spend your days inputting accounts payable and receivables, making journal entries, and producing financial statements, I would hire an accountant. I don't want to do any of those things. I just want to review them and pass on the good news to my investors.

A reputable and experienced accountant is also an important member of your team. If you were to have only three players on your team, your property manager, your attorney, and your accountant would be the most important. Your accountant will be able to keep track of the financial performance of your asset. And you will be able to use the information that they provide you to analyze the property's performance and make adjustments as needed.

Additionally your accountant will be invaluable come tax time. Paying taxes on a large investment like an apartment building is not as simple as picking up a 1040EZ at your local library. It's very complicated.

#4. Mortgage Broker

As we discussed in the chapter on financing, a mortgage broker can be a valuable asset to your investment team. They will have industry contacts that will be able to find you the best loan possible. This can produce a lot of money in interest savings over the long term. Make sure that you use a reputable broker who is licensed, bonded, and insured, and who specializes in large multifamily acquisitions. You can't just go down the road to your local mortgage company. The financing is too complicated.

I have a friend who specializes in putting together large, complicated finance structures for large real estate investments. I utilize his expertise when I'm purchasing a property. His ability to organize financing is well beyond anywhere I'll ever be. I can attest that just by utilizing his services I've saved literally millions of dollars over the years. I'm forever in his debt—oh wait, I'm in debt to the bank, but not to him. He's already been paid. But even my debt to the bank is a good debt because it is part of my asset column, and not a liability.

#5. Commercial Broker

We've discussed the many uses for commercial brokers throughout the book. By now you should already understand the importance of having one on your team. I have one on my team, and he brings deals through my door on a daily basis because of our relationship—because he wants to earn a commission. Never underestimate the power of having someone on your team whose entire pay structure is based on performance.

Besides being a useful resource in your search for investment multifamily deals, your broker can be a wealth of information. Make sure to consult him or her frequently on market conditions. He or she will be able to pull reports on comparable property sales in your market, provide you with rental market comparable studies, and help you determine the capitalization rates in your market. Commercial brokers make their living by having their ear to the ground. Take advantage of that.

#6. Insurance Broker

In life there are two sure things—death and taxes. In multifamily investing the two sure things are insurance and taxes, and then you die. Since the property will be leveraged, the bank will require you to obtain insurance and will give you the specific parameters it is looking for in a policy. They technically own the majority stake of the property, so it's only natural that they want it protected.

The problem is that insurance is extremely expensive. In fact, it is one of the biggest expenses associated with operating your property. That is why you want to get the best deal possible. Your insurance broker will be instrumental in obtaining the best policy for your buck. Soon you will know the lingo, like "limits," "deductibles," "umbrellas," "additional insureds," and, of course, "exclusions."

Again, you can't just call your local agent for this and get the high level of expertise necessary. You will need to find a firm that specializes in policies for large investment properties. The firm you choose must understand the unique needs and nature of multifamily investments. A qualified firm will be able to provide you with quotes from a number of carriers. This will save you money as insurance companies will be competing for your business.

#7. Contractors

If you are looking to purchase a property that will need construction work done, as we did with Edgewood, you will need a general contractor. Make sure he or she is licensed, bonded, and insured. Also make sure that he or she is reputable and experienced in multifamily development. We had a client who picked a local general contractor to build an apartment project of 200 units in a posh area of North Phoenix. Unfortunately, he had little or no experience in building large multifamily projects. Needless to say, the project was a disaster.

Construction supervision is not a responsibility you want to hand over to just anyone. You can check your local government agencies to make sure there isn't any pending litigation against the GC. You can also verify that they are licensed.

If you aren't going to be doing any construction on the property, you can still consult the GC on your team regarding the subcontractors coming out and inspecting the property during the due diligence period. As we have seen, it is important that you have well-qualified subcontractors examine every aspect of the property before you close. Not doing so can cost you dearly.

#8. Appraiser

Your mortgage broker and your lender will most likely assign you a good appraiser. Having an appraiser on your team will help you when you are determining the value of a property for loan purposes. Additionally, he or she will be able to help you identify sales trends in the market. Appraisers, like brokers, make their living by having an ear to the ground. Also, because they are regulated, the information they give you should be accurate.

#9. Architect

A good architect will be valuable to you if you are going to construct new buildings or make additions to your existing property. He or she will be able to help integrate your designs into the existing property. Additionally, he or she will interface with the engineers and make sure that all designs are structurally sound. Choose an architect that has actually designed and worked on apartment buildings and who is also experienced in dealing with the city and state where your property is located when it comes to getting approval for plans. This is a complicated and time-consuming process. Being able to rely on your architect will save you headaches.

#10. Tax Consultant

Taxes are one of the biggest expenses your property will have. Looking to appeal your taxes should be an annual exercise. Each property should be evaluated to be sure that it is in line with the surrounding properties. This process will save you thousands of dollars over the course of your ownership, and your tax consultant will be invaluable.

#11. Environmental Consultants

You do want to take seriously things like mold, lead paint, radon, and asbestos. All of those spell big lawsuits. It is important to have a reputable, third-party company that can identify any issues that a property you own, or a property you are looking to own, may have. Additionally, it will assign what is referred to as a protocol to address the work. Once the work is completed, the company will reinspect the work and issue you a certificate verifying that the issue has been remedied.

When you are purchasing a property, the lender will generally stipulate what company will perform the inspections. But if an issue should arise on a property you already own, you need to address it immediately. You want to know who you are going to use before an incident arises. Research companies and ask around now. Don't wait till you have mold growing inside the walls to start searching for an industrial hygienist.

#12. Engineer

You will want to find yourself a good engineering company. It will be useful in the construction of new properties and often for existing properties, as well as during the time that you own your investment. You can utilize your engineer to perform inspections during your due diligence periods in order to investigate any troubling things you may find in the studies on the physical nature of the property about which the seller may not even be aware. This is what we did when we were looking at the property in Arizona that had expansive soil issues. The report listed it as a problem. I had my engineer come out and examine the foundations, and his findings were key to our decision to walk away from the deal.

If you are planning on adding onto a property as we did with Edgewood, then you will also need your engineer to help with the planning phases. Additionally, if for some reason you find yourself with a property that has physical defects, you will need him or her to assess the situation and recommend a course of action.

Chapter 10

To Infinity—
and Beyond

My kids love the movie *Toy Story*—I have to admit, I do, too. In the movie Buzz Lightyear's key phrase is always "To infinity—and beyond!" It is a call to action. A desire to do whatever is needed to get the job done. I love this phrase because it is forward-thinking. In the movie, Buzz suffers a lot of setbacks. He learns that he can't fly. That there is no intergalactic federation. That he is not the "hero" he thought he was. But the lesson in the movie is that with the right friends, or team, you can accomplish the task before you. Buzz doesn't look back, he looks forward.

Once you put the lessons of this book into practice you will be a multifamily investor. There is no looking back. You have no choice but to move forward. With multifamily investments there are huge responsibilities. Responsibilities to your residents, to your investors, and to your partners. There are also terrific rewards. A solid multifamily investment will be a huge step toward building your wealth and becoming financially independent.

With that bright financial future of yours in mind, I want to close the book with some advice on protecting your assets and yourself. The worst tragedy

I can imagine is for you to take this huge step toward being financially free, only to have to take a step back because of poor planning. We want to look ahead, not revisit the past.

Records

Owning a multifamily investment will require you to be a pack rat. Keep track and file every correspondence you have with residents, lawyers, tax professionals—anyone—regarding the operations of your property. I keep a storage facility literally stacked with boxes upon boxes of documents related to every building I've ever owned or managed. You will thank me if any legal trouble ever comes your way.

Some people ask me how long they should hold on to their records. My answer is: forever. You never know when something might come up. Just recently I had a bogus lawsuit brought against my management company from a resident who was claiming she was injured by an improperly installed ceiling vent. I hadn't managed the property in over five years, and yet here was a lawsuit.

Thankfully, I had kept all the records regarding that property. It was a simple process. I was able to provide proof that the vent was installed properly and that it was an unfortunate incident that led to her injury. The documentation that I was able to provide enabled me to be indemnified from the suit. I didn't even have to pay my attorney fees. The insurance company covered those. We simply weren't at fault. If I hadn't kept good records, I could have been pulled into an awful mess. The burden of proof is always on you. Not the claimant.

Limit Your Liability

They call them limited liability companies precisely because they are companies that limit your liability. I place every property I own in an LLC. The reason is that once a property is placed in an LLC, my other assets are protected from it.

Take the example I just mentioned. The building and management company are separate businesses, with separate LLCs. If the building and the management weren't separate businesses through individual LLCs, the claimant could have sued me based on my entire asset portfolio. Instead, she could only sue my management company. Financial exposure on lawsuits can be extremely high. If you don't have your investments in individual LLCs, all of your properties will be up for damages because instead of your LLC being sued— you are being sued. All of your assets could be at risk and the result could be life-altering. People have had their lives ruined by lawsuits. You can go from financially free to bankrupt in the blink of an eye—if your assets aren't properly protected. Fortunately for me, even with the lawsuit we were facing, the claimant could only go after my management company, which is its own LLC. The rest of my investments and companies weren't even in the picture. Make sure you take the same precautions.

The Sky Is the Limit

Once you have taken the steps to protect yourself and your investments, the sky is truly the limit. You can really step up with confidence and shout, "To infinity—and beyond!" I wholeheartedly believe that multifamily investments are the single best path toward building wealth and financial freedom. The reasons are many:

- Cash flow
- Leverage
- Appreciation
- Tax advantages like depreciation and deductible interest
- The ability to refinance, tax-free
- The protections you can have like LLCs and insurance
- The control that you are able to have over the management performance

I have seen my life and lives of my friends, family, and colleagues change for the better with the power of multifamily investing. I want to see your life change as well. That is why I wrote my first book and that is why I wrote this book. It is the reason I leave my family a few days a month at my own expense to speak with Robert Kiyosaki and the *Rich Dad* team across the country and the world. It is the reason I give you my own personal systems that I've spent years developing. There is plenty to go around.

By reading this book and furthering your financial education, you are making an awesome investment. Put the principles you learn from this book and other *Rich Dad* books into practice, and you will see fruit come from your efforts. Remember that, as Thoreau said, "Wealth is the ability to fully experience life," whatever that may be for you. For me it is spending quality time with my family and friends. I love the fact that I can take my family on vacations and attend all my kids' school and church functions. I'm not constrained by my work. I don't have to punch in and punch out. My money works for me, not the other way around. And it can be the same for you.

Ken McElroy
Principal and Co-Partner of MC Companies

Ken McElroy, co-partner of MC Companies, has over twenty years of senior-level experience in multifamily asset/property management, development, project/construction management, investment analysis, acquisitions and dispositions, business development, and client relations.

Having purchased over $200 million in real estate in the past two years, Ken brings a unique property management perspective to estimate a property's potential value.

Ken is the Real Estate Advisor to Robert Kiyosaki and the Rich Dad organization. In 2004 Ken released the bestselling book *Rich Dad's Advisors: The ABC's of Real Estate Investing*. The *ABC's of Real Estate Investing* is offered as a real estate course throughout Arizona's Maricopa County Community College system. Ken has co-authored several audio programs with Robert Kiyosaki: *How to Increase the Income from Your Real Estate Investments, How to Get Your Banker to Say "Yes!"* and *How to Find and Keep Good Tenants*, which are all available at *www.richdad.com*.

Ken has inspired audiences around the world at Learning Annex events with Robert and Kim Kiyosaki, which have featured speakers Donald Trump, Tony Robbins, Magic Johnson, George Foreman, and others. A frequest guest speaker at Rich Dad events, Ken has appeared on numerous PBS specials and Rich Dad TV with Robert and Kim Kiyosaki. In addition to speaking at the Learning Annex in the United States, Fast Track to Cash Flow in Canada, Infinity Broadcasting, he was a featured speaker at the 2005 National Achievers Congress in Singapore. Ken is also a sought-after speaker at numerous industry events, including AMA's (Arizona Multihousing Association) and NAA's (National Apartment Association) national and regional events throughout the United States.

As host of WS Radio's weekly *Entrepreneur Magazine's Real Estate Radio* program, Ken interviews experts in the real estate, financial, and legal arenas. Ken's guests have included Kim Kiyosaki, author of *Rich Woman; Apprentice* winner and real estate investor Kendra Todd; Rich Dad legal advisor Garrett Sutton; former NBA player-turned-investor Danny Schayes; and bestselling author and speaker Loral Langemeier of *The Secret,* and *Live Out Loud*. An active member of the Entrepreneurs Organization and Arizona's Chapter of Entrepreneurs Organization, Ken held several board positions including president for the fiscal year 2004–2005.

Ken is active within the community and has served on advisory boards for Child Help and AZ Food Banks, where he conducted the largest food drive in the state of Arizona. Ken and his family reside in Scottsdale, Arizona.

The MC Companies are: MC Realty Advisers, LLC; MC Management, LLC; KRM Construction, Inc.; Riverside Builders, Inc.; and Short Term Housing Solutions, LLC.

For more information about Ken McElroy please visit *www.kenmcelroy.com;* for more information about MC Companies, please visit *www.mccompanies.com*.

Link for WS Radio Entrepreneur Magazine's Real Estate Radio:

http://www.wsradio.com/internet-talk-radio.cfm/shows/Entrepreneur-Magazine-Real-Estate-Radio.html.

Bestselling Books by
Robert T. Kiyosaki & Sharon L. Lechter

Rich Dad Poor Dad
What the Rich Teach Their Kids About Money
that the Poor and Middle Class Do Not

Rich Dad's CASHFLOW Quadrant
Rich Dad's Guide to Financial Freedom

Rich Dad's Guide to Investing
What the Rich Invest In that the Poor and Middle Class Do Not

Rich Dad's Rich Kid Smart Kid
Give Your Child a Financial Head Start

Rich Dad's Retire Young Retire Rich
How to Get Rich Quickly and Stay Rich Forever

Rich Dad's Prophecy
Why the Biggest Stock Market Crash in History is Still Coming...
And How You Can Prepare Yourself and Profit From it!

Rich Dad's Success Stories
Real-Life Success Stories from Real-Life People
Who Followed the Rich Dad Lessons

Rich Dad's Guide to Becoming Rich Without Cutting Up Your Credit Cards
Turn "Bad Debt" into "Good Debt"

Rich Dad's Who Took My Money?
Why Slow Investors Lose and Fast Money Wins!

Rich Dad Poor Dad for Teens
The Secrets About Money – That You Don't Learn In School!

Rich Dad's Escape from the Rat Race
How to Become a Rich Kid by Following Rich Dad's Advice

Rich Dad's Before You Quit Your Job
Ten Real-Life Lessons Every Entrepreneur Should Know
About Building a Multi-Million Dollar Business

Rich Dad's Increase Your Financial IQ
Get Smarter With Your Money

www.richdad.com

Bestselling Books by
Rich Dad's Advisors

Sales Dogs
by Blair Singer
Reveal the Five Simple but Critical Revenue - Generating Skills

Own Your Own Corporation
by Garret Sutton
Don't Climb the Corporate Ladder, Why Not Own the Corporate Ladder?

How To Buy & Sell A Business
by Garrett Sutton
Strategies Used by Successful Entrepreneurs

The ABC's of Real Estate Investing
by Ken McElroy
Learn How to Achieve Wealth and Cash Flow Through Real Estate

The ABC's of Building A Business Team That Wins
by Blair Singer
How to Get Rich Quickly and Stay Rich Forever

The ABC's of Getting Out of Debt
by Garrett Sutton
Strategies for Overcoming Bad Debt, as Well as
Using Good Debt to Your Advantage

The ABC's of Writing Winning Business Plans
by Garrett Sutton
Learn to Focus Your Plan for the Business and Format Your Plan to Impress
About Building a Multi-Million Dollar Business

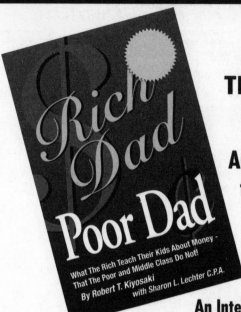

The New York Times writes:

"Move over, Monopoly®...

A new board game that aims
to teach people how to get rich
is gaining fans
the world over!"

WHY PLAY GAMES?

Play often and learn
what it takes to
get out of the Rat Race—
for good!

Games are **powerful learning tools** because they enable people to experience 'hands-on' learning. As a **true reflection of behavior,** games are a **window to our attitudes,** our **abilities to see opportunities,** and **assess risk and rewards.**

Each of the CASHFLOW® games creates a forum in which to evaluate life decisions regarding money and finances and immediately see the results of your decisions.

For more information go to: www.richdad.com

CASHFLOW Clubs

The Benefits of Joining a CASHFLOW Club

Invest Time Before You Invest Money

The philosophy of The Rich Dad Company is that there are only two things you can invest: time and money. We recommend you invest some time studying and learning before you invest your money. The CASHFLOW games offer the opportunity to learn and 'invest' with 'play money' – before you invest real money.

Meet New Friends from Around the World

When you visit or join a CASHFLOW Club (or play the CASHFLOW games on line) you'll meet like-minded people – from all over the world. The world is filled with people with negative attitudes, know-it-all attitudes and loser attitudes. The type of person a CASHFLOW Club attracts is a person who is open minded, wants to learn and wants to develop his or her potential.

Have Fun Learning

Learning should be fun! Too often financial education is dull, boring and fear-based. Many financial experts want to educate you on how risky investing is and why you should trust them. That is not the Rich Dad philosophy on learning. We believe that learning should be fun and cooperative and lead you toward becoming smarter about money so you can tell the difference between good and bad financial advice.

Find a CASHFLOW Club near you:
www.richdad.com

Rich Dad's Wisdom:
The Power of Words

Words are gasoline for your brain. If you improve your financial vocabulary, you will become richer and richer. The good news is: words are free. Which proves, once more, that it does not take money to make money. To expand your vocabulary beyond the financial terms in the glossary you'll find on the Rich Dad web site you might consider acquiring a dictionary of financial terms. When you look up financial words on a regular basis (or look up the definition of a term you hear but do not understand) you may find yourself becoming richer and richer.

An example of the power of words: When people advise you to get out of debt, do they know what they are talking about?

> When you buy a bond, you are buying debt. For example, a U.S. T-bill is a bond – an IOU from the U.S. government. So when you buy a bond you are buying debt...debt that is an asset to you and a liability to the government. So debt can be good. Some of the richest people in the world (as well as financial institutions) get richer because they invest in debt.

When a banker says your house is an asset...ask yourself: Whose asset is it? By definition, assets put money in your pocket and liabilities take money from your pocket. When you look at your bank's financial statement, you can better see whose asset your home really is...

To improve your brain's financial power...improve your financial vocabulary. Words are fuel for your brain!

To learn more about...

Rich Dad's Coaching • Rich Dad's Franchise
Rich Dad Education
Visit: www.richdad.com

Notes

Notes

Notes